El Mouatamid Ben Rochd

American Linguistics
from Whitney to Greenberg

To Noam Avram Chomsky

© 2022, El Mouatamid Ben Rochd
Publisher: BoD – Books on Demand, info@bod.fr
Printing: BoD – Books on Demand,
In de Tarpen 42, Norderstedt (Germany)
Print on demand
ISBN: 978-2-3224-2528-0
Legal deposit: May 2022

CONTENTS

Introduction	7
Language & Linguistics	21
Whitney	39
Boas	43
Sapir	53
Whorf	57
Bloomfield	65
Jakobson	95
Hockett	99
Harris	105
Chomsky	109
Langacker	145
Montague	151
Greenberg	155
Hymes	163
Lamb	169
Labov	175
Pike	185
Grice	193
Peirce	199
Conclusion	205
Appendices	213
Glossary	253
Bibliography	273

INTRODUCTION

Usually, people equate American linguistics with Chomsky's Transformational -Generative Grammar (1957). As a matter of fact there are, at least 3 main notorious trends of language study in the USA, side by side with (or vs.) Chomsky's: William Labov's Sociolinguistics, and Kenneth Pike's Tagmemics.

William Labov's school is concerned with "the language spoken in New York City": how you can determine the identity, the social class of the speaker from his speech (Professor **Higgins**); and most interestingly from his use of the [r] sound or lack of use of this **liquid** (retroflex).

As for Pike and his school, they are very successful translators of the *Holy Bible* into all the languages and dialects of the world, so as to transmit the divine message to every person in his own mother tongue. "No one has any excuse on the day of judgement." Finally, Chomsky's TG school (to which I belong), investigates the nature of language, it considers the simple (or complex) sentence as the unit of language. The sentence is the one constituent that can express an idea, and is the basis for the search for analytic truth.

While the first trend seeks the social classes, the second the message of Christ, the third focuses on the nature of language; its phonetic, syntactic and semantic components, dealt with in the light of a universal set of distinctive features.

In phonetics, the consonants /r, f, b/, for instance, are distinguished from each other by the following features:

Phonetics:

	b	f	r
Coronal	-	-	+
Voice	+	-	+

Syntax:
Sincerity may frighten the boy
Noun: sincerity, boy
Verb: frighten, may
Determiner: the

Semantics:

	Boil	fry	roast
Fire	+	+	+
Direct	-	-	+
Oil	-	+	-

This grammar is closer to Arabic than the others, as it is based on rationalistic analogy and linguistic universals. This reminds us of the dichotomies we find in Sibawaihi's work. Generativists are concerned with the native speaker's competence, as Sibawayh refers continually to "those, whose Arabic is reliable."

The generativists draw a distinction between grammaticality and acceptability as in:

Colorless green ideas sleep furiously

This sentence goes against the **logical features** (or selectional restrictions):

-Colourless vs. green
-green vs. ideas
-ideas vs. sleep
-sleep vs. furiously
(All contradictions)

This was mentioned by Sibawayh in (Gate of Correctness and Acceptability). The examples he gives are: I visited you tomorrow and I will visit you yesterday, I drank the sea and carried the mountain.

As for the dichotomy: deep-surface structure (plus transformations), Sibawayh mentions similar things such as "base" and "preposing, postposing, Pronominalization, internal meaning, transformations". Later, Chomsky recognized the richness of Arabic (Chomsky 1997). [See small potatoes]

Sentence or utterance?

Some linguists focused on the word (Bloomfield), others on discourse (Harris) while the generativists focused on the sentence, which is between the two trends, as the word remains "ambiguous" as long as it is not predicated. For instance *John* can be either the subject, the object of a sentence; it can be vocative, genitive, etc.

Discourse can be summed up in one sentence; books; ideologies, even religions can be summed up in one sentence. Buddhism: 'be patient!', Hinduism: 'everything has a soul', Judaism: 'God chose his people', Christianity: 'the Messiah is the savoir', Islam: 'God is one!'

Discourse can be either spoken or written. Spoken discourse is more alive as it is surrounded by a number of (pragmatic) indices that determine the meaning of the speaker's message and his intention. In the written discourse, you find yourself confronted by writings of an author unknown to you, with all those valuable keys lost.

Even in the presence of the speaker, the time, space, and how are crucial. Discourse analysis remains difficult if not impossible (see English philosopher Patrick **Griffiths**). You have to consider a large number of variables and parameters. It is a difficult mathematical equation.

Robert Le Page believes that the research in discourse and language use is more difficult than the analysis of 'money use'. The latter has so far defeated all attempts made by the economists. You may need, in addition to the text and the pragmatics elements, to know the whole human experience.
[Discourse [context [human experience]]]

While generativists focus on the structure of the sentence, with their infinite number, and their **analytic** truth, literary people (novelists, dramatists and poets) focus on the message and the aesthetic features of the text.

The message of the literary text can be summed up in one simple sentence, as said before, whereas aesthetic, and ecstasy cannot be scientifically quantified. The French say: "les goûts et les couleurs ne se discutent pas!'

Take for instance Shakespeare's play *King Lear*. It is the story of a king forsaken by his own daughters, except the younger Cordelia. He was thinking of keeping his power and ridding himself from the kingly troubles ("Eat his cake and keep it!"). He ended up in the street with the mad and the homeless, suffering the cold and the storm.

The message of this play can be summed up in: "wisdom is in patience." When the king was asked: "are you not suffering the cold and the storm?" His answer was: "when the mind is free the body is delicate." As a **catharsis**, the king learnt who, among his daughters, really loved him and who did not, and also learnt directly what his own people were suffering from, physical misery, psychological pain and social denial.

It was his younger daughter who expressed 'no love' for him when she was asked, who proved to be the most faithful amongst his other (hypocritical) daughters with 'sweet tongues."

Enough literature, another possible way of looking at American Linguistics is to try and encapsulate it under the titles "Bloomfieldians," "Chomskyans" and "Cognitivists." Or again, divide it into Linguistics BC (Before Chomsky), Chomsky and after Chomsky(?) as some would put it.

In fact, American Linguistics started much earlier. The history of linguistics in the United States began with anthropological studies, the goal of which was to discover a greater understanding of humans and their languages. By trying to find a greater 'parent language' through similarities in different languages, a number of connections were discovered (**philology**).

In its beginnings, American Linguistics focused on grammatical analyses and grammatical structure, especially of languages indigenous to North America, such as **Chippewa**, Apache, and multitude .In recent years, the study of Linguistics in the United States has broadened its scope, to include non-standard varieties of English, as well as the question of whether language perpetuates social inequalities.

William Dwight Whitney (1827-1894) was the first US taught academic linguist. He was first a Sanskrit scholar (1880) and the founder of the American Philological Association. During Whitney's professional career he served as president of the American Philologists Society and was also the first editor-in-chief of the *English Century Dictionary* (1889-1891).

The "American Saussure," however is Franz Boas with his famous *Handbook of American Indian Languages* (1911), in which he defended his **relativism** concept, against the absoluteness of ideologies backed nationalisms of Europe of the 30s. Language, race and culture are to be separated.

During the years at the end of the ninetieth and beginning of the twentieth centuries when Saussure was working out his ideas in Europe, synchronic Linguistics was emerging independently, and in a very different style in America, under the leadership of the anthropologist Franz Boas.
(see Sampson 1980)

Then, came towering Leonard Bloomfield with his famous book *Language* (1933). He defended the **mechanistic** discovery procedures and the **behaviourist** background of his linguistic approach. He deals mainly with phonology and morphology, and rejected semantics as unscientific. Charles Hockett suggested three approaches to phonemes and morphemes, which he calls Item & Arrangement, Item & Process, and Portmanteau. Then came pure Structuralists such as Harris and Missionary Linguists such as Pike with his famous **Tagmemics** (Bible Translation Program).

Leonard Bloomfield (1887-1949), professor at the University of Chicago from 1921, founded the Linguistic Society of America in 1924 (see A History of the American Philological Association). Other linguists active in the first half of the

20th century include Edward Sapir and Benjamin Whorf.

From the 1950s, American linguistic tradition began to diverge from the Saussurean Structuralism, taught in European universities, notably with Noam Chomsky's "nativism" and "transformational grammar" in its successive versions, which gave rise to a wide variety of competing theories and ultimately to the 1970s "linguistics wars".

Noam Chomsky (1928-) is often described as the "father of modern Linguistics". He theorized on language from a biological standpoint, referred to as the "**cognitive model**" (of the human brain). He stressed the uniqueness of *man* amongst all other creatures. He states: "how can a system such as human language arise in the mind/brain, or for that matter, in the organic world?" (see Chomsky 1997)

Besides Chomsky's school (with its warring tendencies), you find no less interesting theories such as the American Functional School led by Talmy Givon, and Cognitive Grammar advocated by Ronald Langacker and others. John McWhortter, represents the American school specializing in Afro-American Studies, and Linguistic Typology and Universals led by Joseph Greenberg.

LANGUAGE & LINGUISTICS

As a matter of fact, Language is 'God's secrete gift' to man, so as to ease his action on earth. It is the power of assigning words to objects. The act of naming persons and things by simply uttering a few speech sounds, which stand as symbols for those very persons and objects is indeed a tremendous power. It is crucial in all aspects of man's life and actions on earth. We can only appreciate its value when we start thinking about the enormous difficulties we would have had if we were not given that secret and subtle power of assigning names to objects. Think of the hardship in communication and problems in human relations. When a man wants to communicate with his fellow men about something, he would have had to bring the thing itself in front of them so as to be able to 'talk' about it, be it a *palm tree*, no way but to bring the *palm tree*, be it a *mountain* no way but to go to that *mountain*, be it a *person* no way but to bring the *person* (whether dead or alive) in front of them. It is a paramount hardship that may seriously hinder man's life. Life, at least, the normal one, would have ceased to be without this tremendous **semiotic** power.(Cid, vol. 1, p. 57)

When we observe the movement of the planets by night, we are amazed by their grandeur and exactitude (see "Einstein's miracle!") By opposition, we are able to use our feet to walk, our hands to wave and our tongue to talk. No big deal, it seems. Language is simple and natural, unlike the ecstasy we feel when, we see the amazing motion of the planets and galaxies.

Once psychologist Wolfgang Kohler said: "it is necessary for you, to develop a kind of *"psychic distance"* from the acts that you perform naturally. You have to be able to look at them as it were from the outside, to recognize how amazing they are, before you can begin to try to find out what are the capacities on which these acts are based. It is not a problem when you study, say, physics because, since we are studying something that is external to us, we already have **psychic distance**. We do not move the planets so therefore the fact that the planets move already seems remarkable. But since we are the ones who are doing the speaking, what we are doing sometimes does not seem remarkable, but rather somewhat obvious. However, it is really much more remarkable than the fact that the planets are moving the way they are."

(Mazen Al-Waer, 'An Interview with American Linguist Noam Chomsky', Dept. of Linguistics and Philosophy. MIT. 1980).

As a matter of fact language, is an incredible maze of intricate relationships between sounds, images, patterns, neurological and social relationships. To the extent that despite all researches done in the four corners of the world about LANGUAGE, J.C. Marshal states: "advances in knowledge have only shown even wider areas of _ignorance_ (Marshall 1970, page 241)

The Linguists define their domain as the science of language (read languages in the generic sense). Science or knowledge can be either deductive or inductive. In the inductive tradition of science, four necessary stages are recognized by all researchers,

before reaching any theory about a natural phenomenon. Those are:
- observation
- hypothesis
- experiment
- theory

Tangiers

To try and make things clearer, let me tell you a story. I once met an English student of history at York railway station. He told me about his sister who had gone sightseeing to "Tangiers in Tunisia". I said: "you're welcome to my home in Tokyo"! We both laughed. At first you may think that this student is an idiot. In fact, his knowledge of geography is an acceptable approximation. All inductive (science) researchers are "stupid" like him. They work by approximations.

Take for instance the case of Japanese Dr. Takaki. Not knowing the causes of a sickness that struck the Japanese mariners, he also worked by approximations (hypotheses). He wondered concerning the causes and the cures: was it the cold? a virus? homesickness?, etc., until he found out that it was the "deficiency" in vitamins of the food they ate. Doctor Takaki had to formulate many hypotheses before reaching the conclusion."

Question-Tag
Likewise descriptive linguists work by approximations. They start by observing i.e. hearing an English native speaker's question tag for instance and formulate their hypotheses:

The weather is nice, isn't it?

The first approximation would say: -Locate the verb and copy it to the right of the sentence. If the original verb is affirmative, make the copy negative, and vice versa.

-Locate the subject of the sentence and copy it to the right of the verb.
Result: * The bad boys are in town, aren't the boys?

The second approximation:
-Locate the verb and copy it to the right of the sentence.
-If the original verb is positive, make it negative and vice versa.
-Insert to the right of the verb the pronoun agreeing with the subject in person, number and gender.
Result: *Mary could have arrived, arrivedn't she?

The third approximation:
-Copy the first verb to the right of the sentence, making the copy negative if the original verb is positive and vice versa
-Insert to the right of the copied verb, the pronoun that corresponds to the subject in person, number and gender.

Result: Mary could have arrived, couldn't she?
(see Akmajian & Heny 1975)

Likewise in semantics, the same scenario applies (the binding of reflexives):[*John saw John/*Mary never talks about themselves*].(see Radford 1982)

In scientific research, there are of course debates even conflicts between at least three approaches which are: Deductive, inductive and ecclesiastic. (see **Linguistic Wars**, Newmeyer 1980)

To try and help themselves in this big enterprise, the linguists have come to divide it into a few sections/perspectives: phonetics, phonology, morphology, syntax and semantics to mention but the most important.

Phonetics

Phonetics is the study of the speech sounds. It deals with the speech organs, **articulators**, and air chambers. And divides the speech sounds into **Vowels** and **Consonants**, with open vocal tract and relatively closed vocal tract respectively.

The consonants are seen through three perspectives: place of articulation, manner of articulation and voice. The vowels are trickier to describe. They are all voiced; their place of articulation is palatal. They are described in terms of high-low, front-back dichotomies and rounding of the lips.

The Phoneme

The notion "Phoneme" is essential for the descriptive linguist as a starting point. "The technical term '**phoneme**' is used to indicate the smallest sound feature which is common to all the speakers of a given speech community. These phonemes are analogous to the chemistry chart: the 90 elements (atoms) out of which all substances are made. (see **IPA** chart)

So the "phoneme' can be seen as the minimum "brick in the wall' of language. It plays the distinctive role of demarcation between different words of a language (see O'Connor 1966) e.g. *pit, pet, pat, pot, put* etc. "the phoneme is one of those basic concepts, such as may be found in all sciences, which defy exact [axiomatic] **definition**." (ibid)

The phonemes of different languages may differ, or resemble each other. English has 47 vowels and consonants. Arabic has 28 consonants plus 3 vowels (see Sibawaihi). The phonemes are incommensurable, i.e. a foreign ear hears only a jumble of sounds, which he may try to repeat. The written system tries to unify the pronunciation of each phoneme in the (English) language as if it were uniform among the speakers of American English for say (see Labov). The unified written phoneme (system) overlooks the differences between speakers known as dialects (let alone idiolects). In fact, linguistic descriptions oscillate between '**logic**', **'metaphysics' or even 'prejudice**.' (see Gleason 1969)

"Secondary phonemes of pitch, for instance, mark the end of sentences, and distinguish three main sentence-types, e.g. *John ran away, John ran away? Who ran away?*" (see Bloomfield 1933)

Syllable or Morpheme?

The next unit of language, phonetically speaking, is the **syllable** and semantically the

morpheme. The notion "morpheme" again poses the problem of definition. It may be called the "smallest unit of sound conveying some sort of meaning" e.g. *un-* meaning 'negation', the morpheme *-able*' 'done in a certain way.' The morpheme "is the unit on the expression side of language which enters into relationship with the content side." It consists of one or more phonemes. While the phoneme has no meaning, the morpheme by contrast has one as small as it may be! ('-*y*' as in *tubby* i.e. 'small tub')

Descriptive linguists especially in America (Bloomfield et al) have relied exclusively on these two notions: "phoneme and morpheme" to describe different languages at hand (Indian languages). On the other side stood two other groups: **historical** linguists interested in the changes of language through time (see Grimm) and **comparative** linguists dealing with languages belonging to the same family: Semitic, Germanic, etc (ibid).

Morphology
Languages vary in their morphology (see Chomsky 1997). They are classified as Concatenative and non-Concatenative languages, derivational, inflectional, etc. Morphology studies word formation in each language. As an example American Indian languages are highly inflectional by opposition to Chinese which is hardly so. English is in between. English derivation would yield words such as *sleep* → *sleepless* → *sleeplessness*. It allows also inflections such as "sings" which bears the marks of person, tense and case. Generally speaking, morphology consists of compounding, affixation and category swapping.

Syntax

Syntax studies the acceptable word combinations in sentences, as well as their **hierarchy**: morpheme-word-phrase-sentence. Again languages differ. They are said to be **SVO, VSO, OSV**, etc. In English the most important syntactic relation is word order. For instance, in the sentence *John loves Mary*, the same words, when transposed: subject to object position and object to subject position, viz. *Mary loves John;* the meaning of the sentence changes drastically (dramatically).

Immediate Constituent Analysis (ICA)

For the Bloomfieldians syntax is based on ICA. Each linguistic form is a constituent of some larger form as *John* in the sentence *John ran away*, or independent form, that is not included in any larger or complex form, e.g. *John* for instance in the exclamation *John!*

In the first example, the linguistic form *John* is in included position, and in the second example, it is in absolute position and constitutes by itself a sentence.

Syntactic constructions are defined by Bloomfield as: "constructions in which none of the immediate constituents is a bound form." Immediate Constituent Analysis (ICA for short) is defined as "a term used in grammatical analysis to refer to the major divisions that can be made within a syntactic construction, at any level." (ibid)

[the old man in the corner] [is waiting for the bus]

[the old man] [in the corner] [is] [waiting for the bus]

[the] [old] [man] [in] [the] [corner] [is] [waiting] [for] [the] [bus]

Semantics
Semantics, semiology and semiotics (USA) are used to refer to studies of meaning in general (Ben Rochd 1994). It goes back to the ancient philosophical considerations about meaning. Some trace its etymology back to ancient Greek meaning "to mean". It is derived from Greek *selmantikos* and has to do with the "signs". There is much debate and controversy concerning their definition.

Semantics is the new term used by linguists trying to fix meaning within language, whereas **semiotics** is still used as sign study of general human behaviour, with **iconic figures** such as *Pelé* for "Soccer", *Statue of Liberty* for "freedom", thumb up for "victory and approval", etc.

Syntactic meaning, on the other hand, deals with (co)reference of different noun phrases within a sentence. In a sentence like:

John(1) thinks he(1/2) is clever

Pronoun *he* can refer to the same person or to two different persons (see Chomsky's **Binding** and **Logical Form**).

WHITNEY (1827-1894)

Some people like to consider Franz Boas as the "American Saussure" on the other side of the Atlantic Ocean. In fact the first pioneer of the field is William Dwight Whitney; with his early interest in the **Sanskrit** language, i.e. the ancestor of the Indo-European Language Family, hence the title of his notorious book *Sanskrit Grammar* (1879).

Whitney, William Dwight was born in 1827 in Northampton (Massachusetts). He proved to be a very prolific professor, first of Sanskrit language ever since the year 1854, and comparative Linguistics at Yale University up to 1894. He was an energetic researcher and publisher of a number of works, including editing and translations of the Holy Hindu Book the **Vedas**, written in Old

Classical Hindi language; amazing scholar! He contributed to the establishment of a dictionary of Sanskrit.

He further edited the influential *The Century Dictionary: An Encyclopaedic Lexicon of the English Language* (1891), as well as 1864 edition of *Webster's Dictionary*. This was a tremendous achievement. It was the best 'gift' to the English speakers and learners, ever produced in America and the English world as a whole. His other publications are: *The Life and Growth of Language (1875), Essentials of English Grammar (1877), and Max Müller and the Science of Linguistics: A Criticism (1892). His Selected Writings, (1971)*.

He died June 7, 1894 in New Haven (Connecticut).

Summarizing:

Whitney is not only a pioneer in American linguistics, in fact he is the (unmentioned) scholar who gave an enormous help to those who followed him, both in Vedas Old Sanskrit Studies, but also to the English language scholarship. More importantly, he is the one who opened the door to the "mumbling" new-born science of LANGUAGE.

BOAS (1858-1942)

Franz Boas was a German-born American linguist and **anthropologist** of the nineteenth and beginning of the twentieth centuries; a pioneer of the field research, basing his theory on what will later be dubbed the "Sapir-Whorf" hypothesis (vs. Chomsky's UG). He worked as a professor at Columbia University and was the founder of the first anthropology Departments in the US. He is also a specialist of Native American languages and cultures, besides being a teacher of a number of imminent scholars including Margaret Mead, Melville Herskovits, Edward Sapir, etc.

He was born in Westphalia (Germany) in 1858, to a liberal **Ashkenazi** Jewish family, the son of a merchant, of delicate health as a child, he spent much of his time reading books. As a young man, he considered himself more German than Jewish, only to regret it later on.

At first he was a brilliant student of natural sciences, such as biology, geography, geology, and astronomy. Then his interest shifted to the history of culture. He followed his various intellectual trends at many universities including Berlin, Heidelberg, Bonn, Columbia (NY) and Kiel, taking his Ph.D. in physics and geography at Kiel in 1881.

He was one of the most famous, energetic and politically motivated pre-Chomskian linguists of the early 20th century. He is considered the father of modern American anthropology and the founder of cultural **relativism and determinism."**

His life was a series of non-stop travels. He spent one year as a serviceman in the German army. He then moved to Berlin, and spent one scientific research year in an expedition to the Baffin Island. He became more interested in human sciences than the physical sciences, he previously favoured. He was engaged at the University of Berlin and its museum.

He then decided to move to North America, to focus on the culture and languages of the **Kawkiutl** tribes of Canadian British Columbia. When he stopped for a break in New York City, he decided to stay there until his death in 1942. He was the editor of the magazine *Science*.

His teaching career took him also to Clark University (Mass.) and Chicago, where he worked for the Field Museum of Natural History. Then he took a chair as professor of physical anthropology (1899) at Columbia University (NY). He was also a reporter for the Jesup North Pacific Expedition. This was a most exciting research, in which he was trying to link the aboriginal peoples of **Siberia** and the natives of North America.

(For the crossing of the original Indians from Siberia to America, see Ben Rochd *English*, Bod 2021)

His contributions to natural anthropology went hand in hand, or rather led him naturally, to the study of linguistics in which he excelled, both as a field researcher but also, as a descriptive and theoretical linguist. He established the International Journal of American Linguistics and the American Association for the Advancement of Science.

He published several books and articles such as *The Mind of*

Primitive Man (1911) and a series of lectures on culture and race. This book was much used by the opponents of the new U.S. immigration restrictions based on racial discrimination. "Boas updated and enlarged this book in 1937. Other books by Boas include *Primitive Art (1927) and Race, Language and Culture (1940)*.

Then, he returned to Berlin to deepen the German concept of "kultur". Each time, his ideas stirred big storms concerning race, culture and migration to the United State.

The political context of the 30s was dominated by the spread of Nazi ideology i.e. "white supremacy" based on assumed racial differences. The Nazis of his native Germany even **burnt** his books. His writings were vehemently rejecting Darwinian "**evolutionism**" and their racist carryovers. He also dealt with the multi-aspects of the problems of the migrants, especially the second generation, and its "acculturation" dilemma.

Differences between nations can be explained in terms of the culture and history of each nation. This was behind his moving interest from geography to cultural and linguistic anthropology. He investigated different aspects of the tribes he targeted such as their fishing methods, travels, and atmosphere. As an example, he lived with the **Inuit** tribe, for a certain period of time, learning their language and culture. He believed that each culture is the outcome of a specific history.

By the end of his life, he earned the title of 'father of relativism'. According to him, there are no fixed laws in culture, and no "primitive" or "advanced" nations. Rather, each culture is the outcome of a set of beliefs,

language, customs and arts. For him the world should be considered as a set of culture areas.
According to him, the strict scientific research should begin from CONCRETE DATA collected on the field (like his living with the Inuit tribe) before advancing any linguistic description or theory.

After his retirement in 1936, Boas responded to the **Spanish Civil War** and the steadily growing strength of the **Nazis** in Germany by putting his anthropological ideas about racism into popular journal articles, some of which were collected after his death in *Race and Democratic Society* (1945)." (E. B.)

He also refuted Levi **Straus'** structuralism. Ideologically, he was an anti-Nazi, **communist** and a friend of Russian dictator Stalin to whom he sent letters regularly. He has taught many imminent scholars like **Edward Sapir**, and has left us many books and articles on anthropology, culture and linguistics. His most famous book is his excellent *Handbook of American Indian Languages* published in (1911).

Franz Boas died in New York in 1942.

Summarizing:
Franz Boas is one of the most energetic American anthropologists, turned to linguistics. His contributions were many and include not only anthropology and Linguistics, but also politics and ideology.

Native American languages posed a few problems. One of which is described by Gleason: "Listing of American languages are generally based on the situation at first

European contact or earlier record. This is by no means contemporaneous over the whole hemisphere, but represents a convenient fiction. In many instances there have been great changes since. Not only have languages disappeared, but because of displacement of populations, many are now spoken in areas remote from their earlier location. The map…" (see Gleason 1969)

SAPIR (1884-1939)

Edward Sapir was an American linguist and anthropologist from German origin. His work was focused essentially on culture. He considers "language as a cultural phenomenon par excellence". He is also famous for his Sapir-Whorf hypothesis (elaborated together with his fireman friend Whorf).

Edward Sapir was born in Lunenburg (Germany/Poland) in 1884, in a German **Yiddish** family that migrated to the USA while he was still 5 years old. He became the student of anthropologist Franz Boas at the University of Columbia. Then he spent most of his carrier at the universities of Chicago and Yale, where he met Benjamin Lee Whorf (important for field discoveries).

Sapir developed a new anthropology based on language, following his teacher Boas, in considering language as a cultural fact "par excellence". His study is based on **ethnography**. He conducted several field works on North American populations. From this he elaborated his generalizations. He is also a pioneer in the study of his mother tongue Yiddish.

Language and culture according to him go hand in hand. He initiated the science of anthropology at the intersection between linguistics and ethnology. He is also the inventor of the "**drift**" theory (...) i.e. language moves/changes with time following its own course independently of any external factor. According to him the direction of Language evolution is determined and predictable. (natural syllabic simplification e.g. American *center* pronounced /sene/)

He defended international language **Esperanto** against its "artificiality" foes, as it is, according to him, well rooted in natural European languages. It has widely borrowed forms and vocabulary from originally European stock!

His major book is entitled *Language* published in (1921). He died at the age of 55, in 1939 (Chicago).

Summarizing:

Edward Sapir is an important figure of early American Linguistics, who deepened his teacher's ideas about the connection between language and culture. He also developed the notorious theory of language relativism and determinism together with his friend Benjamin Lee Whorf.

WHORF (1897-1941)

Benjamin Lee Whorf was born in Wethersfield (USA) in 1897. "A descendant of 17th century English emigrants to Massachusetts. In his scholarly work he was an outstanding example of the brilliant amateur. After taking a degree in chemical engineering he began a successful carrier as a fire-prevention inspector with an insurance company in Hartford, Connecticut, and despite several offers of academic posts he continued to work for the same company until his death at the age of 44. Whorf learned lessons from his professional work which encouraged his belief that **world-view is moulded by language**." (see Sampson 1980)

Whorf (the fireman?) became worldwide renown thanks to the

theory which links, in a staunch connection, language and peoples' thinking and perception of the world (**cognition**). He also focused on different languages, and ideas related to **Hebrew**, Mexican, Mayan and **Hopi**.

As a student of Edward Sapir, at Yale University, Whorf deepened the equation of culture and language. This concept was later known as the famous Sapir–Whorf hypothesis. It stresses the concept which says that the structure of each language conditions the way its speakers conceive the world around them. Therefore different language structures correspond to sometimes totally different views of reality. The views of the world are as many as the number of languages of the world. This idea is by no means novel. It is to be found in the works of 18th century

German scholars such as **Wilhelm von Humboldt**.

This theory gained much popularity in North America, as **World War II** was raging in Europe. It was taken first by Edward Sapir and then developed by Whorf in the 40s. It then gained much academic applause. Whorf was mainly fieldwork researcher, especially focusing on American Indian languages. He noticed, for example, the lack of punctuality of some Indians. The cause according to him had to do with the structuring of time (verb tenses vs. aspect, see Arabic) in their languages. He suggested, for example, that the way a people view time and **punctuality** may be influenced by the types of **verbal tenses** in their language.

Whorf's conclusions about the dialectical relationship between different peoples' "languages and ideas" remains controversial, and often ideologically motivated. It ultimately leads to the question of "race and language." Much debate!

As a student of Edward Sapir, he developed the connection between language and cognition (...). The theory became known as the famous **Sapir-Whorf hypothesis**. It is further linked to America's **ethnolinguistic** school.

Benjamin Lee Whorf died in July 26, 1941, in Wethersfield, (Connecticut).

Sapir-Whorf Hypothesis

One can hardly imagine American structuralism without thinking about "Sapir-Whorf hypothesis" (cf. Wittgenstein). It is the hypothesis that says that "language creates thought." Man does not live in a physical real world but rather in a "linguistic world." Every people have their own special world conception, which goes hand in hand with the structure of their language. It is Language that shapes our sensibility of life, in one way or another.

This poses the problem of translation. As an example, you may try and translate early French president utterance: "*La France a élu son président*" or else American president Trump's "*America First*! and lately French president Macron's "*mes amis!*"

into Arabic more or less successfully (Traduttore tradittore).

You may also try to translate the word "*Hamburger*", or "*hot dog*" into Arabic (?) It further poses the problem of the reality of things in the real world and their equivalents in language. *Coal* for instance seems to be a simple and cheap substance, whereas *diamond* is so attractive and expensive. Still the chemist will tell you that they are both representations of the same chemical element.

Sapir-Whorf hypothesis stems from real experiences, lived by the two men. As a fireman, Whorf witnessed that people were careless besides so-called *empty petrol drums* while they were very cautious besides *full petrol drums*. This behaviour led many times to the breaking of fires, as the "empty petrol drums" are more dangerous than the full ones. They contain explosive gases. So Whorf concluded that people live in a linguistic world rather than the real physical one, as the two words "*empty*" and "*full*" played a crucial role in determining their behaviour.

The **Sapir-Whorf** position could be reduced to two principles: **relativism** and **determinism**. By the first one it is meant that people's perceptions of the world as well as the structure of their languages are endlessly diverse. There is no universality. As far as the second principle is concerned, it means that the individual does not choose his world view or even his behaviour, he rather finds himself caught up, so to speak, in a linguistic prison from which there is no possible escape. His mind is moulded by the language he uses.

BLOOMFIELD (1887-1949)

Leonard Bloomfield is the American linguist who produced the most influential books of pre-Chomskian American linguistics including his huge book *Language* published in 1933. It was considered the top contribution to American Linguistics in the beginning of the 20th century. It set the direction for all subsequent works in Descriptive Linguistics.

Bloomfield was born in Chicago (Illinois) in 1887. His education started in Harvard, Wisconsin and Chicago universities. Then from 1909, he started teaching at several universities. He was first interested in Germanic **philology** and descriptive linguistics, which he taught at Chicago and Yale universities.

His main interest was comparative linguistics i.e. tracing the origins of the Indo-European family tree, focusing on phonetics and morphology. Then he turned resolutely to descriptive (scientific) linguistics. He also studied Malayo-Polynesian languages (Tagalog). Then he resolutely turned to American Indian languages, notably the **Algonquian** family.

In his strict scientific approach, he denies any interfering side tracks on language i.e. language structure only, excluding the study of meaning. Still, he did not reject the psychological behaviourist carry over on language, as an aspect of human action and behaviour.

Distributionalism was the outcome of this 'marriage' of linguistics and psychology. It sees language as part of human behaviour that can be studied **inductively**. This approach takes into consideration two major things: stimulus and response. Language, according to him, can be explained in these terms. He explained this concept of his by giving the story of Jack and Jill: "**Jack and Jill** are walking down a lane. Jill is hungry. She sees an apple in a tree. She makes a noise with her larynx, tongue and lips. Jack vaults the fence, climbs the tree, takes the apple, brings it to Jill, and places it in her hand. Jill eats the apple." (see Bloomfield 1933)

Concerning language dialectal variation, "Bloomfield reports that a London cabman did not understand him when he asked to be driven to the comedy theatre. Bloomfield had forgotten himself and spoken the American form of the first vowel in comedy, and this the Englishman could take only as a representative of the vowel phoneme in a word like *car* – so

what Bloomfield was really asking for was the *carmody* theatre, which does not exist."
[For the differentiation between the major two dialects of English: – British RP and American GA: "*In God we trust*", see Ben Rochd 2021b]

The decline of his approach came in the mid 50's of last century, with the advent of Noam Chomsky's TG.

Leonard Bloomfield died at the age of 62 in New Haven (1949).

Bloomfield's *Language* (a Summary)

In his book "Introduction to the Study of Language" (1914), Bloomfield based his work on **Wilhelm Wundt's** psychology, which was the fashion in the first half of the 20th c. Later, in his most famous book "*Language*" (1933), however, Bloomfield decided to free language studies from any extra-linguistic factors. He states: "an exposition which stands on its own feet is more solid and more easily surveyed than one which is propped at various points by another and changeable doctrine." (see Bloomfield 1933)

The study of language
Language plays a great part in our life. Perhaps because of its familiarity, we rarely observe it, taking it rather for granted, as we do breathing or walking. There are circumstances, however, in which the conventionally educated person discusses linguistic matters. Occasionally he debates questions of "correctness" – whether it is "better", for instance, to say *it's I,* or *it's me*. Is a t pronounced in words like often or soften.

The ancient **Greeks** had the gift of wondering at things that other people take for granted. They speculated boldly and persistently about the origin, history, and structure of language. Our traditional lore about language is due largely to them.

In his dialogue Cratylus, Plato discusses the origin of words. This dialogue gives us a first glimpse into a century-long controversy between *Analogists*, who believed that language was natural and therefore at bottom regular and logical, and the *Anomalists*, who denied these things and pointed out the irregularities of linguistic structure.

The ancient Greeks studied no language but their own. They discovered the parts of speech of their language, its syntactic constructions, such as, especially, that of subject and predicate, and its chief inflectional categories: genders, numbers, cases, persons, tenses, and modes.

The Greek generalizations about language were not improved upon until the eighteenth century, when scholars ceased to view language as a direct gift of God, and put forth various theories as to its origin.

The **Romans** constructed Latin grammars on the Greek model; the most famous of these, the work of Donatus (fourth century A.D.) and of Priscian (sixth century A.D.). These remained in use as textbooks through the Middle Ages. The scholastic philosophers discovered some features of Latin grammar, such as the distinction between nouns and adjectives and the differences between concord, government, and apposition.

For the medieval scholar, language meant classical Latin, as it appears in books; we find few traces of interest in any other form of speech. The horizon widened at the time of the Renaissance. At the end of the Middle Ages, the study of Greek came back into fashion; soon afterward, Hebrew and **Arabic** were added. What was more important, some scholars in various countries began to take an interest in the language of their own time.

The **eighteenth** century scholars had not observed the sounds of speech, and confused them with written symbols of the alphabet. This failure to distinguish between actual speech and the use of writing distorted also their notions about the history of language. They saw that in medieval and modern times highly cultivated persons wrote (and even spoke) good Latin, while less educated or careless scribes made many mistakes: failing to see that this Latin-writing was an artificial and academic exercise, they concluded that languages are preserved by the usage of educated and careful people and changed by the corruptions of the **vulgar**.

These misconceptions prevented scholars from making use of the data that were at hand: the modern languages and dialects, the records of ancient languages, the reports about exotic languages, and, above all, the documents which show us successive stages of one and the same language, as for instance **Anglo**-Saxon (Old English) and modern English, or Latin and the modern Romance languages. The doctrine of linguistic decay discouraged systematic study of this relation, since the changes which led, say, from Latin to modern French, were viewed as haphazard corruptions.

The more familiar languages of Europe fell into three groups by virtue of close resemblances within each group: **Germanic** (English, Dutch, German, Danish, Swedish) Romance (French, Italian, Spanish) Slavic (Russian, Polish, Bohemian, Serbian)

Outside the tradition of Europe, several nations had developed linguistic doctrines, chiefly on an antiquarian basis. The Arabs had worked out a grammar of the classical form of their language, as it appears in the **Koran**; on the model of this, the Jews in Mohammedan countries constructed a Hebrew grammar. At the Renaissance, European scholars became acquainted with this tradition; the term *root*, for instance, as a designation for the central part of the word, it comes from Hebrew grammar. In the Far East, the Chinese had gained a great deal of antiquarian linguistic knowledge, especially in the way of lexicography. A Japanese grammar seems to have grown up independently.

In India, the language of the Rig-**Veda** (sacred texts of the Brahmin religion) grew antiquated, the proper way of pronouncing them, and their correct interpretation, became the task of a special class of learned men.

We find the Hindu grammarians extending their interest from the Scriptures to the upper-caste language, and making rules and lists of forms descriptive of the correct type of speech, which they called *Sanskrit*. In time they worked out a systematic arrangement of grammar and lexicon. Generations of such labor must have preceded the writing of the oldest treatise that has come down to us, the grammar of **Panini**. This grammar, which dates from somewhere round 350 to 250 B.C., is one of the greatest monuments of human intelligence. It describes, with the minutest detail, every inflection, derivation, and composition, and every syntactic usage of its author's speech. No other language, to this day, has been so perfectly described.

In the **eighteenth** century, Englishmen in India transmitted knowledge of Sanskrit, which became part of the equipment of European scholars.

2) The use of language
Writing is not language. It is just recording language by means of visible marks. In order to show the usage of language, Bloomfield takes into account two major things: stimulus and response. For

the equation: Language =stimulus-response, see the Story of Jack & Jill. Man utters many vocal noises; under certain kinds of stimuli, and his fellows, hearing these same sounds, make the appropriate response.

The mentalist theory supposes that the variability of human conduct is due to the inference of some non-physical factor, a spirit, will or mind that is present in every human being. This spirit according to the mentalists view is entirely different from material things and consequently follows some other kind of causation. Whether the speaker will speak or what words he will use, depend upon some act of his mind or will. This mind or will does not follow the (cause-effect) patterns of succession of the material world, we cannot foretell his actions.

On the contrary, the materialist (or mechanistic) theory believes that the variability of human conduct, including, speech, is due to the fact that the human body is a very complex system. Man's actions, in this theory, are part of cause-effect sequences exactly like those which we observe in the study of physics and chemistry. We could foretell a person's actions if we know the exact structure of his body at the present time, or better still from his birth stage. Man's nervous system is a very complex conducting mechanism. A change in one part of the body results in a change in the whole body (PT). The nervous system is a trigger-mechanism.

3) Speech communities

A speech community is a group of people who interact by means of speech. It is the most important "leader" of the social group. Many other phases of social coherence, such as economic, political, or cultural groupings depend upon language for their existence. The child learns to speak like the people surrounding him, to become a native speaker of that language (**mother tongue**). Speech communities differ greatly in size. Latin and Greek were spoken by millions of people around the Mediterranean Sea during the first century of the Christian era. Dutch and German form one single speech community, but are no longer mutually intelligible.

English children born in wealthy families will speak "good" 'standard English', less fortunate children will speak "bad" English i.e. **cockney** or vulgar e.g. *I have none vs. I haven't any, I ain't got none*. Local differences exist, a person from Chicago, for instance will use '*ah*' vowel in "*father*" instead of the common 'a' vowel as in "*man*." He is said to speak "high-class" English. The differences depend on economic, education, social class and occupation. Craftsmen, merchants, engineers, lawyers, physicians, artists, seafaring men, criminals; each group has their own secret dialect. In some countries (France, Germany) opposite ends cannot understand each other.

4) The languages of the world

In the course of time, many languages of the world disappeared. Some are known from their written records only. English is the most widely spread. It is related to German, Flemish, etc. but differs from all of them. It was originally brought about by invaders to the British Isles: Angles, Saxons, Jutes (15th c.) Then it split into different dialects, due to migration. German split into low and southern high. Yiddish is spoken in Poland and Russia. Icelandic German differs from the rest and is spoken by a few thousands. Other nations came in the same (linguistic) area; the Goths, Vandals, Burgundies, Lombard, etc. Their long historic separation from each other made their languages mutually unintelligible.

Bloomfield considered also a wide range of different languages such as Bohemian, Pashto, Sanskrit, Southern Arabic, Hieroglyphic, Christian Coptic, Hausa, Zulu, Tartar, and Mongols. On the American continent, there are some unrelated 50 unstudied languages, Eskimo, Mohican, Apache, Navaho, Hopi, Mayan, Aztec, etc. many among them have died.

5) The phoneme
The phonemes of a language are not speech sounds, just phonetic features, which the speakers have been trained to produce and

recognize in the current of actual speech. They are indefinitely varied. Different persons speak differently, and we recognize their voices, (even on the phone). The phonetician deals with the constant sound wave and ignores the meaning of what is being said. If we hear "*man*" spoken by two English speakers we should say that it is the same speech-form. But if the speaker is Chinese, the two instances may mean two different things (words). The pitch contour of "man" may mean either "deceive" with a rising pitch, and "slow" with a falling pitch. The phonetic features are either distinctive or non-distinctive. In American English the phoneme /t/ in water, butter, is often reproduced with the tongue tip against the alveolar ridge becoming /d/. In England it is interpreted as distinctive e.g. din and tin. The vowels in words like hot became closer to those in words like far. As an example see the story of the "car-mody theatre".

For the scientific transcription of language we need a system with a one-to-one correspondence between sounds and their representative symbol. For each phoneme a specific symbol is given (see **IPA**).

6) Types of phonemes
There are two main types of phonemes: noise sounds (stops, trills, spirants) and musical sounds (nasals, laterals, vowels). Stops exist in every language. In English they are produced from lips, teeth and velum. The trill is an apical (tongue tip) with many strokes against the gum, as in Italian, Russian and Scottish *rain*. American English is well known for voicing /t/ as in *water* (see Ben Rochd 2020c). In French nasalized vowels as in *un bon pain blanc*. Vowels are trickier in their description. They involve no

closure, friction or contact. They all belong to the palate, with vibration of the vocal cords. Their table is as follows:

	FRONT	BACK
HIGH	i	u
HIGH MID	e	o
LOW MID	ɛ	ɔ
LOW	a	ɑ

[See the 7 keywords of English (Ben Rochd 2021)]

7) Modification

The phonetic modifications (vs. modality) can be realized in various ways. Duration and length of time, are found when the speech organs are kept in contact. This must be captured by a phonetic sign. Long vowel in German *beet* (flower bed) as contrasted with *bett* (bed). The stress and loudness with which the sound is produced are called secondary phonemes: stress, secondary stress e.g. *vegetarian* is understood only when pronounced with the right intonation, regardless of its syllables. The pitch is also a crucial feature as in: *this is my parking place e.g. it is not my fault it is your fault.*

The schwa occurs in unstressed syllables as in : '*contest vs. con'test*. Intonation also plays a role in formal vs. familiar, polite, derogatory utterances. Differences in pitch go hand in hand with the scope of hand gestures. A question vs. a statement e.g. *it's ten o'clock!*, rising v falling. In English when passing from silence to a voiced stop, e.g. *bay, day* the voicing is gradual, and contrary when passing from sound to silence as in *ebb, egg*.

8) Phonetic structure

According to Bloomfield language serves as stimulus-response bond between speaker and listener. This whole operation depends on the "phoneme" as it is the unit of speech. Some constraints do apply to the structuring of the sequence of phonemes in each and every language. In English the two phonemes [VELAR NASAL] and [ALVEOLAR FRICATIVE] never begin an utterance (vs. Malay?) Final clusters in English cannot be ss tt, nor initial. The examples given by Bloomfield are as follows: bet-s test-s text-s. Middle syllables and all final position combinations occur as in: *glimpsed strips, ten nights*. Phonology is responsible for the possible structuring of phonemes in a given language (UG). A single phoneme such as –s is meaningful, e.g. *book-s*.

9) Meaning

Again, for Bloomfield "meaning" can be defined in terms of "stimulus -response." Meaning has to be "scientific" and if at all "demonstrative." We can teach someone the meaning of the French word "*Pomme*" by handing him an apple, or pointing to it, or its translation in his own language. Usually people utter words, the referent of it is not present in the context of the conversation. This he calls "displaced speech." Bloomfield gives the example of the beggar who utters "*I am hungry!*" and the housewife gives him food. Mentalists and mechanists have differed in what concerns "the learning of meaning." The first group believes that the speaker goes through a mental process: thought, concept, image, feeling, act, etc. for them language is "the expression of ideas and feelings." By opposition, the mechanists believe that the mental images, feelings, etc. are "popular terms for body movements."

Words are tricky. They do not have a one-to-one relation with the real world. Someone can point to a man and say: "*there goes a fox*," in the metaphoric sense. The word "*cats*" can include lions, panthers and tigers. Unlike exact chemistry definitions, e.g. the word "*salt*" which is defined as "Na Cl", no way can we do the same with words such as: *love* or *hate*. (see Leech 1974)

10) Grammatical forms

According to Bloomfield language consists of phonemes, which are grouped into "forms." Again, it is the stimulus-response bond between speaker and hearer. For instance, in *John ran* and *John fell*, and *John*, we deduce that these three forms are partially alike, since they all contain *John*. In the partly alike utterances, there are two types of *John*, and the parts which are not partly alike: *ran* and *fell*. In other cases, some forms cannot stand by themselves, but rather belong to a greater linguistic form e.g. *John*, *Bill* and *Dan*, we may expect *playing*, *fighting*, but not –*ing* in isolation. These are called constituents of complex forms e.g. *poor John ran away* consists of a hierarchy of constituents.

The meaning of a morpheme is called "**sememe.**" It is part of the lexicon. The ordering of the forms of a language are of crucial importance. They make up its grammar. Bloomfield suggests 4 ordering forms: order (*John loves Mary*), modulation (*b-r-e-a-d*), phonetic modification (*didn't*) and selection (*John run*).

11) Sentence types
A linguistic form is either dependent or free. *John* is

dependent as in John ran away, or independent as in exclamation John! Sentence types are usually marked by **taxemes** (grammatical features), such as the use of secondary morphemes and selection. Intonation marks the end of the utterance, exclamation, or question. Two or more independent sentences can form one single (complex) sentence e.g. *it's ten o'clock & I have to go home*.

Interrogative substitutes can be of the form: *who? With whom? Who ran away? With whom was she talking?* There is a further distinction between Full sentences and Minor sentences. English has actor-action sentences e.g. *John ran away*. The other is a command e.g. *Come! Be good!* Minor sentences are interjections e.g. *oh! Dear me!* Bound forms never occur as full sentences e.g. *boyish, tubby*. Bloomfield considers the word as the "minimum free form." (see Bloomfield 1933).

12) Syntax

Grammar contains morphology and syntax. In syntax, Bloomfield takes into account three main factors: **order**, **selection** and **immediate constituents** e.g. *John loves Mary, *John come Mary*. He considers also what he calls "**sandhi** forms" such as French contraction loses the (e) vowel before a word starting by a vowel e.g. *l'encre* "the ink." (see Bloomfield 1933)

Selection and agreement are also crucial. They determine case, e.g. *Bill runs fast*. *Bill* is in nominative position, *me* class in accusative and *to me* serves as oblique (goal).

13) Morphology

Bound forms i.e. words and parts of words, are subject to modification and modulation. Languages differ drastically in morphology (see Chomsky 1997). The word classes are: secondary (free forms), compound (more than one), derived (one free form), primary (more than one bound), morpheme-words (one single free morpheme). Take for instance the word *gentlemanly*, it is a derived secondary word but not a compound word, because of the bound morpheme –ly. In secondary derivation bound forms derive plural nouns, feminine and past tense, as in *glass-es*, *actr–ess* and *work-ed*.

14) Morphological types

The Bloomfieldian concepts of morphology are freely applicable to Arabic. Like English, Arabic has free forms which can stand alone, and bound forms, which cannot be isolated such as u: "they" in *daxal-u:* "they entered."

Gleason's Assessment of the Bloomfieldians' legacy.

There are many DIFFERENCES between the different Bloomfieldian trends. Gleason states: "even within the relatively narrow circle of American descriptive linguistics, viewpoints have been **far from homogeneous**. There have been three great classic formulations: Boas' Handbook of American Indian Languages (1911), Sapir's Language (1921), and Bloomfield's Language (1933). These show wide differences together with important shared basic convictions." (see Gleason 1969).

As a summary of the Bloomfieldian School, we can state the following guidelines:

1) American structuralism stemmed from Anthropology

2) It focused on American Indian languages
3) It relied on Behaviourist psychology
4) It excluded semantic study as unobservable.

JAKOBSON (1896-1982)

Roman Osipovich Jakobson is a famous Russian born American linguist and an encyclopaedic scholar, both in Europe (Prague School) and North America. Together with Prince Nikolaj S. Trubetzkoy, he founded the Functionalist School of Prague. Jakobson extended the structuralist Saussurean concepts to include many different perspectives of language study.

Jakobson was born in Moscow (Russia) in 1896. In the beginning of his career, he became professor of Russian at the Higher Dramatic School of Moscow in 1920. In 1928, with his colleagues of the Prague School, he departed from the pure synchronic structuralist ideas of Swiss Ferdinand de Saussure, to consider the linguistic elements both synchronically and as they change with the course of time. His revolutionary ideas were exposed in his first books including: *Remarques sur l'évolution phonologique du russe comparée à celles des autres langues slaves (1929)*, "Comments on Phonological Change in Russian Compared with That in Other Slavic Languages".

Jakobson started his teaching career at Masarykova University (Czech Republic) in 1933, where he taught Russian philology and Czech Medieval Literature (1936). The rise of Nazism in Europe, compelled him to flee first to the northern European states to teach successively at the Universities of Copenhagen, Oslo, and Uppsala (Sweden) as a visiting professor.

Then in 1941 he fled to the United States. He taught different subjects, including Slavic languages, general linguistics and the art of poetics at Columbia University (New York City) from 1943 to 1949, and at Harvard from 1949 to 1967.

"Big scholar Roman Jacobson's" reach was enormous. His academic knowledge includes Slavic languages, literature and traditions, diachronic, communicative and general linguistics, poetics (see Haj Ross), aphasia, child language, phonological studies (Distinctive Features), and so on and so forth. This can be inferred from the titles of his most influential works viz. *Kindersprache and Aphasie und allgemeine Lautgesetze (1941), Studies in Child-Language and Aphasia, Preliminaries to Speech Analysis (1952), and Fundamentals of Language (1956), The Sound Shape of Language(1979)*. (Encyclopœdia Britannica)

<u>Summarizing</u>:

Russian American linguist Roman Jakobson was indeed encyclopaedic, and deeply influenced Morris Halle, Noam Chomsky and Haj Ross amongst many others in the United States. He died July 18, 1982, in Boston, (Massachusetts).

HOCKETT (1916-2000)

Charles F. Hockett is an American linguist, famous for his structural approach to language. He was born 17 January 1916 in Columbus (Ohio). He was the 4th child of Homer Carrey Hockett, himself professor of American history at Ohio State University. Hockett Junior, enrolled at the State University of Ohio at the age of 16, and was interested in linguistics starting from 1933. He obtained his Masters in Antic History at the age of 20.

Then, he moved to Yale University. As a student of Edward Sapir, he started his study of anthropology. He got his PhD in 1939 for his work on Potawatomi American Indian language. His thesis "Patowatomi Phonemics, Morphophonemics and Morphological Survey", was published by the International Journal of American Linguistics, and remains a reference for that language.

During the Second World War he served as a linguist (translator?) and obtained the rank of lieutenant, serving in China, Bengal and Japan.

In 1946, he started a new academic career by joining the prestigious University of Cornell (New York), as professor of linguistics.

Amongst his innovative ideas about language I& A and I&P and the dichotomies "overt editing" and "covered editing."

"An important article by Hockett (1954) forms the best starting-point. In this article, Hockett surveyed what was then the state of grammatical theory, and distinguished 3 very general concepts of linguistic structure. The first, to which he gave the label *Item and Arrangement* (abbreviated IA), is the one which had been dominant since the mid-1940s; it was on the merits and possible defects of this viewpoint that his argument accordingly turned. The second and third, to which he gave the labels *Item and Process* (IP) and *word and paradigm* (WP), were alternative approaches which had, in the immediately preceding period, been given rather less attention. Hockett argued that there were enough criticisms of IA to suggest that IP, in particular, deserved more serious consideration." (see Lyons 1970)

"The terms "surface structure" and "deep structure" come from Hockett (1958: 246) and were not used in the earlier accounts of transformational grammar (…)This is substantially the same conclusion as that reached by Hockett, in his distinction between "cover editing" and "overt editing," where he writes "editing in the internal flow is *covert editing*…In certain formal circumstances covert editing is thorough, and overt speech is unusually smooth. Much more typically, what is actually said aloud includes various signs of *overt editing* (Hockett 1967: 936) " (ibid)

Charles F. Hockett died in Ithca (New York) November 3, 2000.

Summarizing:
Charles Hockett is one of the most brilliant Bloomfieldian linguists. His anthropological and descriptive approach to language was based essentially on IA (Item and Arrangement), IP (Item and Process) et al. The "Item and Process" approach is actually a

precursor of "Transformational Grammar."

HARRIS (1909-1992)

Zellig Harris is a Russian American linguist. He was born in 1909 in Balta (Russia). His fame came from his book *Methods in Structural Linguistics* (1951) and another no less fame by being the direct teacher of Noam Chomsky, with whom he shared linguistic and radical political ideas.

Harris' parents migrated to the United States in 1913 when he was still a child. He was educated at the University of Pennsylvania, where he received his B.A., M.A., and Ph.D. (1934). He began teaching in the same University in 1931 and became Benjamin Franklin Professor of Linguistics in 1966.

His book *Methods* established his scholarly reputation as a **theorist**. In his subsequent work on **discourse** analysis, Harris suggested the use of transformations as a means of expanding descriptive analysis across sentence boundaries. Since He was Noam Chomsky's teacher, some have considered him as the initiator of the TG Revolution rather than his student Chomsky. In fact the two had different ideas and different contexts. For the teacher "transformations" were the link between actual sentences, for the student "transformations" were the leap between abstract deep structures and actual concrete sentences. Those were two different transformational grammars.

Summarizing:

Chomsky's teacher Zellig Harris was a linguist and a politician, who brought American structuralism to its logical summit, to the extent that some refer Transformational

Grammar to him rather than to Chomsky (see Sibawayh). He suggested dealing with language structures beyond phonemes, morphemes and sentences to their limit i.e. to **discourse**. At any rate, the notion "transformation" is due to him as its initiator in the American linguistic tradition.

Zellig Harris died May 22, 1992, in New York.

CHOMSKY (1928-)

Noam Avram Chomsky was born in Philadelphia (December 7, 1928) from a Jewish Ukrainian Ashkenazi family. His father was a scholar of Hebrew and Arabic. He himself recognized having studied Arabic grammar (the classics of Ajerumiya and Sibawayh).
His world-wide fame came with the publication of his first monograph *Syntactic Structures* (1957) and his political activism as an opposing militant outspoken against the Vietnam War and the policy of President Nixon (Black Listed). As a young man, he intended to travel to the Middle East to try and reconcile Jews and Arabs, but his family dissuaded him from doing so. Instead he was encouraged to stay home and study, with Zellig Harris.

His studies of linguistics were initiated by his father then by Zellig Harris, of Pennsylvania University. He obtained his degrees swiftly one after the other: BA, Masters and PhD (1955). He is life professor at MIT and visiting professor at the University of Arizona.

He is almost a century old now, but still very active in politics. See his analysis of the Russian invasion of Ukraine which could "bring the world to its end" by a nuclear 3rd World War, according to him. God forbid!

Chomsky revolutionized the academic world by his Transformational Generative Grammar in 1957. He broke with the dominant American descriptivist Bloomfieldian school of his time, which advocated that "language is a set of verbal habits established by means of training

and experience"; i.e. the building of mental synapses.
(See Skinner)

By opposition, Chomsky advocated the idea that "man is unique." Language forces us to this conclusion. He sates: 'Any progress toward this goal will deepen a problem for the biological science that is already far from trivial: how can a system such as human Language arise in the mind-brain, or for that matter, in the organic world, in which one seems **not to find** anything like the basic properties of human language?'
(see Chomsky 1997)

The human baby comes to the world with an **innate** formal capability for building and understanding natural language, whichever language he is exposed to regardless of typology, tone, VSO, etc. This is why all children of the world learn their mother

tongue in relatively **rapid** and **uniform** stages. They hear a chunk of their mother tongue and then are able to generate an infinite number of utterances that they have and may never hear from their elders.
(see Jonathan Miller)

A further "revolution" of Chomsky's is to suggest that language is a two-story building; what he calls **deep** and **surface structures**. The first is for **sound** and the second for **meaning**. The link between the two is a set of rules (or principles) named **transformations**. He moved then to argue that these transformational (rules) are universal and hence his **UG (Universal Grammar)**.

Chomsky dominated the 2nd half of the 20th c. with brilliant works such as Syntactic Structures (1957), Aspects of the Theory of Syntax (1965), Language and the Mind

(1972), Lectures on Government and Binding (1981), and the Minimalist Program (1997). He was surrounded by bright students, such as Richard Kayne, Ken Hale, Morris Halle, James McCloskey, Friz Newmeyer, Haj Ross, Joan Bresnan and many others coming from the four corners of the World viz. Huang, Rizzi, Mazin al-Waer, Fassi-Fehri, etc. the list is almost endless, stretching from Osaka to Los Angeles.

In his pre-minimalist program, Chomsky suggested two models: either one consisting of a system of rules, or one consisting of principles.

First model
The subcomponents of the rule system consists of PS rules, Lexicon and Transformations (& islands)

1) PS rules
    S → NP-VP
    VP → V-NP

NP→ Det- N

2) Lexicon
"a lexicon includes a list of all the words of a language, together with a specification of their idiosyncratic phonological, morphological, syntactic and semantic properties, as in:

Eat: V, + [NP-- NP] "
 +[animal]+[edible]
(see Radford 1982)

3) Transformations (& islands)
Transformations operate from an input towards an output e.g.

The boy hit the ball → the ball was hit by the boy

Transformations are often constrained by what is sometimes referred to as "ISLANDS" e.g. the A-over-A. "Consider the following paradigm (a) *he will emerge out of which tunnel?* (b) *Which tunnel will* *he emerge out of --? (c) *of which tunnel will he emerge out--?* How is it that we can prepose NP and PP in some structures like those above, by wh-movement, but not PP (c)? We might seek the answer to this question in terms of the following constraint proposed by Chomsky; A-over-A constraint: no constituent of category A can be moved out of a larger containing constituent of category A (=of the same type)." (ibid)

Second model

The subsystem of principles: X-bar, Government, Theta, Binding, Case, Control, Bounding

1) X-bar

"there is some empirical evidence (from coordination, *one-*Pronominalization, etc.) in support of the existence of categories intermediate between lexical and phrasal categories, so that we might replace the Phrase Structure categories of X AND XP by the richer system of X-bar syntax in which more than one *phrasal projection* of lexical categories is recognised (i.e. X, X-single-bar, X-double-bar, etc.)." (ibid)

2) Government
Government is sometimes equated with c-command.
"X c-commands Y iff (=if and only if) the first branching node dominating X dominates Y, and X

does not **dominate** Y, nor Y, X."
(ibid)

3) Theta

"Another group of linguists would argue that dictionary entries for verbs should also contain a specification of what are known as *thematic relations*. Consider sentences such as: (a) the ball rolled to the bottom of the hill, (b) John rolled the ball to the bottom of the hill. In (a) and (b) the *ball* has two entirely distinct syntactic roles: in (a) *the ball* is the subject of *rolled*; whereas in (b) it is the direct object of *rolled*. And yet one might argue that in the two sentences, *the ball* in each case has the same semantic or thematic role- namely that of the entity which undergoes motion." (ibid)

4) Binding
Besides syntax, Chomsky's model deals with problems of reference. Andrew Radford states: "At this point, we turn away from syntax for a moment to consider briefly the role of semantics in the model proposed by Chomsky…the syntactic component of a grammar has the task of specifying which combinations of words in a language do or do not form grammatical sentences, whereas

the semantic component of the grammar is concerned with specifying what those sentence-structures generated by the syntax actually mean…"
(ibid)

To express (co)reference relations amongst the noun phrases of a given sentence a complex system of indices is used as in:

John(1) thinks he (1/2) is clever
He (1) thinks he (1/2) is clever

Co-indexing expresses the co-reference condition of two noun phrases and random indexing lack of co reference otherwise.

Chomsky (1981) suggested a series of binding conditions:

- a) An anaphor must be bound in its governing category
- b) A pronominal must be free in its governing category
- c) A lexical NP must be free always.

That can be exemplified in:
John(1) hurt himself(1)
John(1) hurt him(2)
John(1) hurt Fred(2)

5) Case

"Personal pronouns in English may have as many as three distinct forms –cf. the paradigm: *he-him-his*. These forms are traditionally referred to as different *cases* () of the pronoun: thus, *he* might be called the *nominative* case form of the pronoun, *him* the objective form, and *his* the *genitive* form." (ibid)

6) Control

Control concerns the empty category PRO, suggested in (Chomsky's Pisa lectures, 1980, p. 22). "Chomsky assumes that in sentences like: John tried *to frighten* Mary, the italicised infinitive complement has an empty pronominal which he designates as PRO () He further maintains that PRO, although abstract, must contain inherent person, number and gender features." (ibid)

7) Bounding

Bounding concerns a set of constraints on NP and Wh-movements e.g. SUBJACENCY CONDITION. "EXTRAPOSITION from NP whereby a certain type of complement of a generally indefinite nominal can be detached from the NP containing it, and *extraposed* (= moved to clause-final position). For example we might say that the italicised post nominal prepositional phrase in (a) can be moved into clause-final position in (b) by application of EXTRAPOSITION: a critical review *of his latest book* has just appeared → a critical review – has just appeared *of his latest book…** the fact that a critical review – has just appeared is very worrying *of his latest book*... (is ungrammatical). Chomsky's answer is to propose the following constraint; SUBJACENCY CONDITION: no constituent can be moved out of more than one containing NP – or S-node in any single rule-application." (ibid)

Logical Form

"The concept of logical form has two meanings. Within the philosophical tradition, the concept developed in opposition to "grammatical form" thus, the grammatical form of the sentence "the King of France is bald" was taken to be, basically, the surface structure, but the logical form, Bertrand Russell suggested in a famous and influential article, would be something like: there is one and only one entity that is the King of France and that entity is bald" (thus false, because there is no such entity). In contrast, "the Queen of England is visiting Morocco" would be true or false depending on whether that entity, which does exist, in fact has the property "visiting Morocco."

Within linguistics this term has a related but somewhat different meaning. We assume, as a matter of empirical fact, that **language** faculty is an identifiable component of the **mind**, and that in its mature state, it has the form of a generative procedure that generates the structural descriptions of sentences. These structural descriptions interact with (at least) two other systems of the brain/mind: the articulatory and perceptual systems; other conceptual systems. We further assume that each structural description contains a representation of phonetic form (PF), which is the level at which the former interaction takes place and includes all information relevant to it; and a representation of logical form, which is the comparable level of interaction between the language faculty and conceptual systems. In fact, the properties of linguistics "logical form" (LF) are often surprisingly close to those proposed for the semantic analysis of natural language on other grounds, but the nature of LF is an empirical matter, just like the nature of PF. On the matter of "strong evidence in support of the UG hypothesis," I find it hard to answer. It would be as if someone asked: what is the evidence that there is a genetic basis for the fact that the embryo becomes a human rather than a bird, the evidence is so overwhelming that no contrary hypothesis is even entertained by any sane person. The same is true in the case of the "UG hypothesis," which is just a special case of the other. It is transparent, and not argued among serious people who have thought about facts, that the knowledge that a person has is vastly undermined by the evidence available to them. Thus, the sentences of this letter may have never been produced in the history of the human race, but every person who knows English understands them (at least, in the sense of identifying the words, phrases, their interrelations, etc., if not in the sense of following the discussion of logical form). Everyone who knows English knows that in the sentence "John's father thinks that the idiot will never pass the exam," the phrase "the idiot" may be referring to John, but cannot be referring to "John's father; and in "John thinks that the idiot will never pass the exam." It must be referring to someone unmentioned in the sentence. The same is true in every other language, as far as we know. These facts are known completely without evidence. No child ever makes an error about these matters, and is corrected by its mother; actually, the facts were not even noticed until a few years ago. There is a huge mass of evidence of a similar nature, and the only coherent possibility is that this information is a property of the language faculty, in effect, not fixed by experience. UG is just the theory of the initial state of the language faculty. People, who question the "hypothesis of UG," unless they are mystics, must be confused about something. () There is no debate about the issue among people who understand

what is being discussed, nor could there be."
(Professor Chomsky, personal communication)

Distinctive features

Transformational generative grammar was primarily concerned with syntax, but phonology got also its share from this huge enterprise. "Two major statements concerning distinctive features approach have been made: one by Roman Jakobson & Morris Halle, in Fundamentals of Language (1956), the other by Noam Chomsky & Morris Halle, in the Sound Pattern of English (1968).The Jakobson & Halle approach set up **features** in pairs, defined primarily in acoustic terms (), but with some reference to articulatory criteria. Examples of their features include vocalic vs. non-vocalic, consonantal vs. non-consonantal, compact vs. diffuse, grave vs. acute, nasal vs. oral, discontinuous vs. continuant, strident vs. mellow, flat vs. sharp/plain and voiced vs. voiceless. The emphasis in this approach is firmly on the nature of the oppositions between the underlying features involved, rather than on the description of the range of phonetic realizations each feature represents." (see Crystal 1985)

Chomsky's co-workers and their "linguistics wars"

Amongst the top students of Chomsky's are Richard Kayne, Joan Bresnan and Kenneth Hale.

Kayne (1944-)
Richard Kayne is a brilliant Chomskian linguist. He earned his BA in mathematics at Columbia University (New York) in 1964. He studied linguistics at MIT, where he got his PhD in 1969, obtained his docteur es letters (linguitique) Univetsité de Paris 8 in 1976,

Syntaxe Française: le cycle transformationnel. He taught at the Université Paris 8 from 1969 to 1986, then at MIT from 1986 to 1988, then at City University of NY from 1988 to 1997. He contributed very nicely to French linguistics, comparative (Romance) linguistics and to the development of generative grammar in France and Europe. His speciality is comparative French and Italian syntax (see Ben Rochd 1994). His latest Anti-Symmetry Theory superseded X-bar syntax and was borrowed by Chomsky in his latest TG version (Minimalist Program).

Kayne's sweet *French Syntax* (1975) [a summary]

This is a very nice book of French Syntax, within the Chomskian paradigm. It contains the following chapters:

1: the leftward movement of tout/tous
2: clitic placement
3: the fair-infinitive construction
4: clitic placement in the fair-infinitive construction
5: reflexive/reciprocal clitic placement
6: the transformational cycle

In chapter 2, Kayne discuses a transformation he calls **Clitic Placement**.

 "Direct NPs in French normally follow the verb:
(1) Marie connait mon frère
Marie knows my brother
If the subject is a personal pronoun, however, the corresponding sentence is ungrammatical:

(2) *Marie connait nous

Rather, the pronoun appears to the left of the verb:

(3) Marie nous connait.
Marie knows us

In section 2.2., we shall consider the best way to account for such facts within a transformational grammar. We shall argue in favour of a movement transformation, to be called '**Clitic placement**,' which would prepose object pronouns to the verb under certain conditions. One environment in which such a rule would be inapplicable is the ne…que construction. If the direct object pronoun is the 'focus' of ne…que, it remains in the usual object position and may not precede the verb:

(4) Marie ne connait que nous
Marie knows only us
*Marie ne nous connaît que

What interests us here is the fact that many personal pronouns have a different shape in a sentence like (3) than in one like (4)." …

For the justification of the transformation Cl-Pl, broadly speaking, we have the choice of compiling either the phrase structure rules or the transformational component, or both. One possibility would be to say that sentences containing clitics are generated as such in the base, that is, that the PS rules should be extended so as to allow the Clitic pronouns to be generated in their surface positions. We could then claim that sentences (4/16), for example, had a deep structure essentially identical to its surface structure; that is, that an NP object appeared at neither level. An obvious difficulty with this analysis is the problem of stating subcategorization restrictions, since, restricting ourselves to the simplest cases, direct object clitics co-occur only with verbs that also take direct object NPs. Thus connaitre, but not partir, must be assigned subcategorization " _NP":

(17) Marie connait Paul
(18)*Marie part Paul
Marie is going away Paul."

Summary and Conclusion:

Kayne discusses the interactions between different transformations in French.

"in summary, then the transformations Se-PL, Fl/A-Ins/FP, when applied in cyclic fashion, interact in such a way as to generate the superficially complex array of sentences shown in (63), where the order of application is given by (a) Se-Pl→Fl, (…). This accounts for the varying position of the "antecedent" of se (sometimes to the left, sometimes to the right), as well as for the superficially asymmetric distribution of à (…) as discussed earlier.

(63)
Le hasard a fait se connaitre Jean et Marie
Jean s'est fait connaitre à Marie
Jean s'est fait arrêter par la police
Jean s'est fait passer pour fou."
(page 439)
 (see Kayne 1975)

Joan Bresnan (1945-)
Joan Wanda Bresnan was born in 1945. She is the inventor of the theory of **Lexical Functional Grammar.** She graduated from Reed College in 1966 in philosophy, and got her PhD from MIT in 1972. She first worked with Chomsky and focused on **Wh-movement.** "Chomsky's solution to this problem was the radical proposal that, contrary to appearances, wh-movement is a cyclic rule. He adopted a proposal made by Bresnan (1970) that wh-movement involves moving the wh-phrase into the complementizer position of a clause roughly speaking, the

clause initial position occupied by that or whether. This position, known as COMP, has the status of an 'escape hatch' for movement; movement to or from the COMP position does not violate the TSC or SSC." (see Harlow 1995)

She was often at odds with her professor Noam Chomsky, facing him with different propositions. She soon departed from transformational grammar to deepen her own ideas about language. She published The Mental Representation of Grammatical Relations (1982). She dealt with English, but also **Bantu** and Australian languages. She worked on **Optimality** theory and statistical linguistics, which led her to her Lexical Functional Grammar, based on linguistic Typology.

She earned the Gugenheim Fellow in 1975, and served as president of the famous Linguistic Society of

America in 1999. She was Honoured as Festschrift in 2005. From 2009 to 2012 she was visiting professor at Freiburg Institute for Advanced Studies. She was elected a Fellow of the Cognitive Science Society in 2012, and lifetime member of the Association for Computational Linguistics in 2016. Finally, she has a Position at Stanford, and teaches at both University of Massachusetts at Amherst, and MIT.

In December 16, 2018, Sanford listed **44** books and papers of hers.

Ken Hale (1934-2001)
Kenneth Hale was a brilliant multilingual professor of linguistics at MIT. He was born in Evanston (Illinois). He studied at the University of Arizona. His dissertation was written about **Tohono** language, Bloomington Indiana University (1959). He did much for the protection of Native Americans'

languages and political rights (**American Indian Movement**).

Together with his wife and son, he travelled to Australia where he conducted much field research about Australian aboriginal languages. He first taught at the university Urbana Champaign (Illinois), then the University of Arizona (Tucson) and then joined Chomsky and Halle at MIT in 1967.

He spoke several languages, besides English, Jemez, Hopi, Walbiri and Arabic. He played a crucial role in the establishment of universal grammar and its relationship with linguistic variation.

He also contributed to comparative and cultural linguistics. He helped educating natives of exotic (American) languages, such as Ellavina Tsosie Perkins, Paul Platero (Navajo), Ofelia Zepeda (Papagoand)

Laverne Masayesva Jeanne (Hopi). He was a regular member of Navaho Languages Academy and ANAS. He also directed the lexicon project together with Samuel Kaiser. This had much influence on Chomsky's later **Minimalist Program**.

Here is a sample of his work on Australian aboriginal languages: "the grammar of **Walpiri**, an aboriginal language of central Australia, exhibits a number of properties which have come to be associated with the typological label '**non-configurational**,' including among other things, (i) free word order (ii) the use of syntactic discontinuous expressions, and (iii) extensive use of null anaphora. Free word order is amply exemplified in any sufficiently large body of Warlpiri narrative or conversation...(the) sentence below may be rendered with the subject, object, and verb in any order.

 Nagarrka-ngku ka wawirri panti-rni
 Man   ERG AUX kangaroo spear
                          NONPAST
 The man is spearing the kangaroo."
               (Hale, 1983)

Multilingual, brilliant and humane Professor Kenneth Pike passed away October 8, 2001.

Halle (1923-2018)

Morris Halle was an "old MIT" American Phonologist. He was born in Leetonia from Jewish family, that migrated to the United States. He was professor emeritus at MIT. He was one of the pioneers of generative phonology. Together with Noam Chomsky, he produced the most influential book The Sound Pattern of English (1968). He was a member of the Linguistic Society of America. He spoke fluently at lest six languages which were Hebrew,

Yiddish, Lepton, Russian, German, and (Arabic). He supervised Malling's dissertation on Arabic.

Maling ()
Joan Maling is an American linguist working at MIT, specialist of Arabic metrics. She worked under Morris Halle.

Summarizing:
"After the war of 1939-45, American structuralism moved into its generative phase. Thereafter, it was the canon to take a language forms from matrix arrays of features, combine and order them in sequences, perhaps transform the interim results, and so generate the permissible sentences. The triggers were rules, of strictly defined input and environment, arranged in their own recognized orderings. The concept was clearly analogous to historical change and its handling by 'laws' (). Conversely, a historical shift could be presented as here

the insertion, there the deletion, of a rule or else as a change in rule ordering or context. The catchword was 'simplification.' Among the practitioners were Morris Halle (1962), Robert D. King (1969) and Paul Kiparsky (1965)." (see Collinge 1995)

Chomsky had many other brilliant students; i.e. Joseph Aoun, McCawley, Lakoff, Jackendoff, etc. Unfortunately, amongst themselves, there was not always "flowery and rosy" relations. Sometimes, the disagreements reached unimaginable hate heights. Friz Newmeyer narrates: "It is hard in retrospect to appreciate the vehemence with which the debate between **generative semanticists** and partisans of the **Extended Standard Theory** (interpretivists) was carried out in the late 1960s and early 1970s. At times, its heat grew so intense that even in print the rhetoric exceeded the bounds of normal partisan scholarship—witness Doughtery's (1974:267) description of a paper of **McCawley's** as "Machiavellian" and George **Lakoff'** s (1972f: 70L) accusation that Chomsky "fights **dirty** when he argues. He uses every trick in the book." As can easily be imagined, the discussion sessions after conference papers provided an arena for far stronger sentiments. The high point (or low point) surely followed the presentation of George Lakoff's "Global Rules" paper at the 1969 Linguistic Society of America meeting, when for several minutes he and Ray **Jackendoff** hurled amplified **obscenities** at each other before 200 embarrassed onlookers." (see Newmeyer 1981)

LANGACKER (1942-)

Ronald Langacker is an American linguist, and professor at the University of California at San Diego. He is the founder of **Cognitive Linguistics**. He was born in 1942 in Wisconsin, his studies were done at the university of Illinois. (Wikipedia)

"Cognitive grammar is a radical alternative to the **formalist** theories that have dominated American theoretical linguistics in the second half of the 20th century. Instead of an objectivist semantics based on **truth conditions** or **logical deduction**, it adopts a **conceptual semantics** based on human experience; i.e. our capacity to construe situations in alternative ways, and processes of imagination and mental construction. Conceptualist semantics makes possible an account of grammar which views it as being inherently meaningful (rather than an autonomous formal system). (ibid)

Ronald Langacker is a brilliant American linguist, still working. He obtained his PhD from the University of Illinois in 1966, and from then up to 2003 he was professor at the University of California (San Diego) and president of the International Association of Cognitive Linguistics. He worked first within the Chomskian Government-Binding framework (see, On Pronominalization and the Chain of Command 1969). He is recognized as the founding father of cognitive linguistics and cognitive grammar.

Many philosophers since Plato have taken man's ability to know as the characteristics distinguishing him from all other animals. The very name of him being, *Homo sapiens*, means "man the knower."

If one asks: "**what is knowledge?**" he has raised the central problem of a major field of philosophy, i.e. **epistemology**. But there is also a very important psychological aspect to knowledge, and that is where the philosophy of mind becomes relevant. It is often claimed, for example, that knowing that something is so entails believing that it is so; and the nature of belief lies clearly within the province of the philosophy of mind. Since a person does not lose a belief when he is not consciously attending to it, the approach to belief most in favour today is to treat it as a disposition, which, like all such, comes to open expression only sporadically. Other psychological phenomena falling within the area of the cognitive are attention, sense perception, understanding, memory, inference, and doubt. The view that each of these requires a subjective experience has been effectively refuted in Wittgenstein's writings, one of the seminal thinkers of modern Linguistic Analysis. Remembering that the oven is still turned on may consist in nothing but getting up in the middle of a conversation, going over to the oven, and turning it off, all the while animatedly continuing the conversation. But exactly why this is called "remembering that the oven is still on" is not clear. Perhaps the best that can be said is that there are analogies between such instances of remembering and other, more self-conscious instances. It is the task of the philosophy of mind to examine, classify, and analyze the relations among such phenomena." (ibid)

Langacker 'Cognitive Grammar' is a highly innovative theory of linguistic structure that has been articulated and progressively developed ever since the year 1976. In stark contrast to modular approaches, it regards language as an integral facet of cognition, and grammar as being inherently meaningful. It presupposes a 'conceptionalist' account of linguistic semantics that properly recognises our capacity for construing the same conceived situation in alternate ways. With an appropriate view of meaning, all grammatical elements are reasonably attributed some kind of conceptual import. Grammar is thus considered 'symbolic' in nature: it reduces to the structuring and symbolization of conceptual content." (ibid)

<u>Summarizing</u>:
Langacker, a former Chomskian student, has a developed a new (?) conception of language, that disregards, pure Bloomfieldian structuralism and Chomsky's

autonomous syntax. It suggests that "every bit and parcel in language" is directed towards or simply, is "meaningful" and has direct access to human consciousness.

MONTAGUE (1930-1971)

Richard Merett Montague was born in Stockholm (Sweden) in 1930. He then moved to the live and work in the US. He is considered as one of the most brilliant American philosophers, mathematicians and linguists, who challenged Noam Chomsky himself, if only for his short life (41 years only!). His major impact on linguistics is his **Natural Semantics Theory**. It is based on logical mathematics, predicate logic, and intensional logic amongst other concepts. For him, natural languages and formal languages (programming) can be treated in the same way and by the same logical approach.

He states: "there is in my opinion no important theoretical difference between natural languages and the artificial languages of logicians: indeed, I consider it possible to comprehend the syntax and semantics of both kinds of language within a single natural and mathematically precise theory. On this point I differ from a number of philosophers." (see Universal Grammar 1970)

In his short academic life, he managed to produce several influential papers:

"Universal Grammar" (1970)

"English as a Formal Language" (1970)

"The Proper Treatment of Quantification in Ordinary English" (1973).

Montague's grammar can represent the meaning of quite complex sentences compactly.

The type of the syntactic categories in his grammar are (t) denoting a "term" (a reference to an entity) and (f) denoting a "formula." So "terms" "formulas", "predicate", "function", etc are among the tools he uses in his syntactico-semantic analysis.

"The important thing here is that the meaning of an expression is obtained as a function of its components, either by function application () or by constructing a new function from the functions associated with the component. This compositionality makes it possible to assign meanings reliably to arbitrarily complex sentence structures, with auxiliary clauses and many other complications."()

Richard Merett Montague died in Los Angeles, (USA) in 1971, at the age of 41.

Summarizing:

In his short but brilliant academic life Montague defended the hypothesis that says that you can deal with natural languages and the artificial languages of logicians in a single natural and mathematically precise theory.

GREENBERG (1915-2001)

Joseph Harold Greenberg is a modern American linguist. He specialized in **African languages** and gained his world-wide fame with his **Language Universals**. As a student of Franz Boas, he contributed an important unified anthropology, based on **mass comparisons**.

He was born in 1915 in New York (USA). He studied at Columbia University under the supervision of Franz Boas. He earned his B.A. in 1936 and his PhD in **anthropology** in 1940 from Northwestern University in Evanston (Illinois) under the supervision of Melvile Herskovits. He joined the U.S. Army from 1940 to 1945. He, then joined the University of Minnesota (1946–48) and Columbia University (1948–62), and later Stanford University (1962–85) as professor of anthropology.

He published his reference book: *Studies in African Linguistic Classification* (1955), *The Languages of Africa* (1963). This work has been controversial ever since its publication. Some consider it as the best study carried out on African languages. But some believe that it is just a "copy" of earlier classifications done on African languages by German Diedrich Westermann.

According to Greenberg, African languages can be **classified** according to **sixteen families**, he later reduced them to just four: Niger-Congo, Afro-Asiatic, Nilo-Saharan and Khoaisan, which are then subdivided further. His results are based on **mass comparison** and similarities existing between the vocabularies of these languages. The results sought by Greenberg were to arrive at some **genetic** connections (dangerous!). His results are somewhat generally accepted by comparative linguists.

Where Greenberg succeeded best and earned more applause is his studies on **Language Universals**. He published "Some Universals of Grammar with Particular Reference to the Order of Meaningful Elements."(1966).

He suggested forty-five **universal word orders** and **inflectional categories**. This work of his was solidly based on the **data** collected from some **thirty** languages. His universals touched not only on grammar but on pragmatics and logical meaning as well, such as the **conditional proposition** of the form "If A, then B" ("implicational universal").

He was the editor of *Universals of Language* (1963) and *Universals of Human Language* (1978).

"Many of Greenberg's universals provide statistical correlations between the basic word-order of a language and other features of its grammar. " (see Smith & Wilson 1980)

"The minimal contrast rule, was suggested by some remarks of Greenberg (). He pointed out that there was a greater tendency to change a feature from, rather than to, its marked value in word-association data.

FEATURES STIMULI MAJOR CONTRAST MINOR CONTRAST DOUBLE CONTRAST

+/-Child	man	woman 62	boy 8	girl 3
+/-female	woman	man 53	girl 9	boy 1
	boy	girl 70	man 5	woman 0
	Girl	boy 60	woman 5	man 1

[Stimuli with major, minor, and double contrasts as responses with their percentage of occurrence in word association norms].
(see Lyons 1970)

"In its original form, this parameter characterizes the relative order of subject, verb, and object, giving rise to six logically possible types, namely SOV, SVO, VSO, VOS, OVS, OSV. (see Chomsky 1997)" (see Comrie 1995)

"While Chomsky claimed that the study of any one language in its deep structure would by definition be as study of universals, Greenberg set about looking for universals in an empirical way, by examining the grammars of a sample of languages from numerous language families. He found that while absolute universals, such as having the vowel /a/, were trivial to the deeper understanding and functioning of language system, a large number of 'implicational' universals could be discerned that related the functioning of seemingly unsuspected ways." (see Koerner 1997)

"Quantitative studies have introduced the notion of Statistical Universals, i.e. constants of statistical kind, such as a **ratio of use** between different structures. Implicational universals are generalized statements of the form ' if X, then Y', e.g. if a language has a word order of a certain type, it will also have a verb structure of a certain type." (see Crystal, 1985)

[See also Kayne in Ben Rochd 1994)]

Summarizing:

Greenberg (1915-2001) has deeply renewed African and American-

Indian language typology, as well as his ideas about language origin. He gained world-wide fame with his LANGUAGE UNIVERSALS THEORY, based on mass comparisons, which are generally agreed upon unlike his genetically based mass comparisons.

Joseph Harold Greenberg died in 2001 in Stanford (California).

HYMES (1927-2009)

Dell Hathaway Hymes is an American sociolinguist, anthropologist, and folklorist. His work is essentially concerned with American Indian languages of Northwest Pacific (British Columbia). He set a **Speaking Model**. He became famous for his Communicative Competence (vs. Chomsky's competence).

In sociolinguistics, Hymes' Speaking Model is a mnemonic technique used as a tool contributing to identify and characterize the constant parameters of linguistic interaction. Hymes believes that to speak proper language, you need not only to master the vocabulary and grammar but above all, and in addition to those purely linguistic competences, the context of each word you use.

So as to clarify his idea Hymes constructed the acronym **S-P-E-A-K-I-N-G** which stands for: setting (& scene), participants, ends, acts sequence, key, instrumentality, norms and genre. He suggested another mnemonic acronym for his theory in French viz. **P-A-R-L-A-N-T** which stands for: participants, acts, raison (or results) localization, agents, norms, and tone. This groups together the 16 components that he had previously divided into 8 sections.

Hymes' model contains **16** components, which help in the analysis of the different aspects of discourse: the form of the message, the content, the time of enunciation, the transmitter, the receiver, the destined, the goals, the finalities, the tone, the channels, the genre, etc.

To fix the "Native Speaker's Communicative Competence"

Hymes suggests a few linguistic parameters among which the following:

Setting and Scene
By setting, Hymes refers to all the physical circumstances surrounding a given discourse: time, place, i.e. the room chosen in the house, the psychological context, the cultural environment, the degree of formality, the degree of seriousness amongst family, friends, or colleagues.

Participants
By participants, Hymes means both the speaker and the hearers. There is however a distinction between the audience targeted by the speaker, and those who are not. A grand dad may tell the boys among his grand children a story targeting them, but his grand daughters may also hear the story although they were not meant to do so.

Ends

Ends stands for the speaker's intention as well as the results on the audience. A story can be narrated for entertainment, moral lesson or, remembrance of an event or a dear person, such as a grandma.

Sequence Act

Sequence act refers to the chronological order of the event, such as telling a story after a toast at the dinner table. The audience may interrupt the story sequence, by questions, remarks, or jokes. At the end of the story the group may be astonished, impressed or happy and applaud.

Summarizing:

Hymes globalizing approach came as a challenge to Chomsky's pure linguistic theory. It was much appreciated by English Language teachers (**ELT**), as it provided them with the adequate technology for their foreign language teaching.

LAMB (1929-)

Sidney Lamb is an American linguist and follower of Hjelmslev's Copenhagen school.

Sampson (1980) states: "Much more interesting than Hejlmslev's own work (Glossematics) in the development it received at the hands of the American Sydney Lamb (1929), formerly of the University of California at Berkley and since 1964 at Yale, and Lamb's follower Peter Reich, of the University of Toronto. Lamb () begins by listing a few simple, common types of relationship that obtain between units in a language. One relation is that of **alternation**, where a given unit at a 'higher' (near meaning) level is realized (either indifferently, or depending on circumstances) as one of several alternative elements at a 'lower' (near sound) level; if

we accept that *go* and *move* are close synonyms, then we may say that a single 'meaningful-unit' LOCOMOTE is realized alternatively as the lexical item move. (The notion of 'meaning-unit' or, in Lamb's terminology '**sememe**', symbolized here by small capitals, is of course philosophically speaking very naive and crude; and indeed the hole notion of a stratum of 'content-substance' is highly questionable – cf. Uldall 1957, …since Lamb's treatment of meaning is no worse, though it is no better, than Chomsky's or almost any other linguist's, and I wish to concentrate in the more positive, worthwhile aspects of Lamb's work.)
Similarly, the units *under* and *beneath* might be viewed as alternative realizations of a semantic unit LOWER THAN. The opposite alternation is neutralization, in which a single lower-level unit represents either of

two or more higher-level units. Thus the lexical item *move* may represent the meaning-unit LOCOMOTE, but it may alternatively stand for the specialized meaning which it has in *I move that these minutes be accepted* – say, PUT A MOTION. Alternation and neutralization are both what Lamb calls 'or-relations': element A at one level corresponds to element B or element C or element D at another level."

"Lamb's approach to language is also referred to as 'relational grammar' "I use the term 'relational grammar' to cover the theory initiated by Hjelmslev and H.J. Uldall and developed by Sydney Lamb And Peter Rich. Hjelmslev and Uldall called their theory 'Glossematics' or 'immanent grammar', and the term 'Stratificational grammar' is associated with lamb's work; none of these latter names seem particularly apt, and the suggestion that Hjelmslev and Lamb belong to distinct 'schools' is quite misleading. A further source of potential confusion stems from the use in the last few years of the tem 'relational grammar' to denote a variant of Chomskyan Linguistics which lays more stress than Chomsky himself does on concepts such as 'subject' and 'object': this latter theory has not seemed to me different enough from Chomsky's to warrant separate treatment in this book (and Reich has established a prior claim to the term 'relational grammar')." (see Sampson 1980)

Summarizing:

Sidney Lamb was first a follower of Danish linguist Hjelmslev Glossematics. He tried to give it a more realistic push, with an emphasis on the study of alternations of 'sememes' i.e. units of meaning. This school is also known as 'relational grammar' or 'Stratificational grammar'.

LABOV (1927-)

Besides mathematicians, philosophers and linguists, America produced brilliant sociolinguists such as William Labov.

"William Labov was born on December 4th 1927 in Rutherford (New Jersey). He studied at Harvard in 1948 from which he got his BA and worked as an industrial chemist from 1949 to 1961, before turning to linguistics. For his Masters thesis he completed a study of the Change in the Dialect of Martha's Vineyard, which was presented before the Linguistic Society of America to great acclaim. Labov took his PhD at Columbia University in 1963. He taught at Columbia from 1964 to 1970 before becoming a professor of linguistics at the University of Pennsylvania in 1971, which, by that time, had become the Mecca for the discipline. He became director of the University's linguistic laboratory in 1977. The methods he used to collect data for his study of the varieties of English spoken in New York City, published as *The Social Stratification of English in New York City* in 1966, have been influential in social dialectology." ()

In the late 1960s and early 1970s, his studies of the linguistic features of African American Vernacular English (AAVE) were also influential in the sense that he argued that AAVE should not be underestimated as substandard but respected as a variety of English with its own grammatical rules, although speakers of AAVE should be encouraged to learn standard American English for interactions in society at large. He is also famous for his seminal studies of the way ordinary people structure narrative stories of their own lives.

"The study of variables is one of the central tasks of any investigation of the dialects of American cities. Applying the statistical methods of modern sociology, linguists have worked out investigative procedures sharply different from those of traditional dialectology. The chief contributor has been William Labov, the pioneer of social dialectology in the U.S. The basic task is to determine the correlation between a group of linguistic variables—such as the different ways of pronouncing a certain vowel—and extralinguistic variables, such as education, social status, age, and race. For a reasonable degree of statistical reliability, one must record a great number of speakers. In general, several examples of the same variable must be elicited from each individual in order to examine the frequency and probability of its usage. Accordingly, the number of linguistic variables that can be examined is quite limited, in comparison with the number of dialectal features normally recorded by traditional fieldworkers in rural communities; in these situations, the investigator is often satisfied with one or two responses for each feature." (E.B.)

Labov stresses the need for African American Vernacular English (AAVE) to be respected and given its right status as a recognized variety of English, with its own grammatical rules. Still, the (AAVE) speakers should also be encouraged to learn standard American English so as to achieve two goals: communication, and social promotion. His study seminars gained much fame, especially his gatherings of people to tell their own linguistic experiences.

With his Yiddish background (Hebrew-German dialect of Eastern Europe), William Labov was a first hand witness of language change in time, place, social contexts and human attitudes. His 1963 Masters written about the sound change in Martha's Vineyard and later his PhD thesis on sociolinguistics strata in New York City (Harlem) was the starting point of modern linguistic variation theory. Labov's intent was to develop an empirical, rigorous, and universal (?) approach to language as it is actually used, in real context.

His sound change studies led to develop a UG (...) in modern phonology with universal and language-specific constraints. As an example his study of the /t/d/ sounds variations and different auxiliary renderings have been used for the study of several (non-English) languages.

His primary focus was on the vowel system of American English (New York et al.). It has had an immense impact on subsequent dialectology studies. His survey studies and modern technological techniques based on computer aided technology, culminated in the publication of his notorious work: *Atlas of North American English*.

Labov's gender and class-based models of language variation is the key to understanding the prestige gained by his approach and theory. His works include *Language in Inner City, Studies in Black English Vernacular* (1972), *Sociolinguistic Patterns* (1972) and *The Atlas of North American English* (2006). In the late 1960's, he broke with the hard psychological "armchair linguistics' of the Chomskian paradigm, to achieve an adequate field research in language. He was mainly concerned with so called 'Black American English', using the speech of the clerks working in stores; how they pronounced or dropt certain sounds. Their speech idiosyncrasies usually reflected their social condition; their voicing of /t/, their retroflex /r/, auxiliaries, etc. This represented the birth of a new discipline known as **'Social Dialectology.'** It was a scientific study of dialectology based on the speech of the black inhabitants of New York City.

William Labov noted the differences and similarities in English pronunciation. It is well known that English has a major split between Received Pronunciation (RP) and General American (GA). The latter is noted for its back vowels and /t/ voicing, as can be heard in American pronunciation of the

Dollar's Motto *"In God We Trust"* and *"New York City"* (pronounced /ga:d/ and /sidi/) (see Ben Rochd 2021).

In grammar Black American English is well known for its (illogical) double negation e.g. *I ain't never done nothing*! and the dropping of present tense 3rd person suffix –s e.g. *he do it*. These features probably come from the south and are due to the old slavery days, as can be found in New Orleans, well-known for its 'soul food' and 'soul music' (John Lee Hooker).

William Labov's Methods of sociolinguistic research can also remind us of English Robert Le Page's *Acts Of Identity'* (1980) in his investigation of social variables: race, class, gender, age, and education. Each linguistic variation in pronunciation or grammar corresponds to a specific regional dialect or social strata. Usually, differences in speech determine people's group awareness and help the speaker in identifying, joining or rejecting, the visa-à-vis as potential 'friend or foe!'

Also, in any language, a special dialect is used as a means for social promotion as is testified in Bernard Shaw's play *Pygmalion*. For finding a job, the dress and the speech make up the success of the individual, even the idiot.

In England itself, you have those differences in grammar and pronunciation, e.g. a couple discussing whether to use *cut* or *cutting* in "my nails need--", the word *poor* pronounced /poːr/ by some English speakers, to the extent that someone wondered: "Do the English speak English?" Not to forget Leonard Bloomfield's "car-comedy theatre" anecdote!

Summarizing:

William Labov used special methods for collecting his data of the varieties of English spoken in New York City, especially African American Vernacular English (AAVE), the speakers of which must not be underestimated, but should also be encouraged to learn standard American English for better interactions and socioeconomic benefits.

PIKE (1912-2000)

There is another famous and innovative structuralist trend in America led by Kenneth Pike. It is known as **Tagmemics** Linguistics. Its primary goal is **Missionary Work**. It aims at converting the tribes of Central and South America to Christianity. It has what is known as the Summer Institute of Linguistics (SIL). It has realized so far a big deal, and only a few thousand languages remain to be dealt with, so as to transmit the Holy Book to everyman in his own mother tongue! (see Sampson 1980).

Kenneth Pike is a brilliant American Missionary linguist and anthropologist. His fame is due to his studies of the aboriginal languages of many parts of the world ranging from Mexico, to Ghana, Nigeria, Australia, and the

Philippines. He is the innovator of the Tagmemics school.

Pike was born June 9, 1912 in Woodstock (Connecticut). He studied theology at Gordon College (B.A., 1933) and in 1935 he joined an organization dedicated to linguistic study of rare and unwritten languages, for the sake of universal Bible translation. This group evolved into the **Summer Institute of Linguistics**, with himself as its   president from 1942 to 1979. He travelled to several parts of the world for his missionary endeavour, including Mexico (see **Mixtec language**). This experience boosted his linguistic expertise. He obtained his PhD from the University of Michigan in 1942, and started teaching there, from 1948 to 1977, and then became the chairman of its linguistics department.

Tagmemics is an outcome of Bloomfieldian Immediate Constituent Analysis, together with its psychological theory, based on general human behaviour. Hence the title of his book: *Language in Relation to a Unified Theory of the Structure of Human Behavior* (1954).

According to Pike an *emic* unit is 'an entity seen as "same" from the perspective of the internal logic of the containing system, as if it were unchanging even when the outside analyst easily perceives the change'. An *etic* unit is 'the point of view of the outsider as he tries to penetrate a system alien to him; and it also labels some component of an emic unit, or some variant of it, or some preliminary guess at the presence of internal emic units, as seen either by the alien observer or as seen by the internal observer when somehow he becomes explicitly aware of such variants through teaching or techniques provided by outsiders.

Kenneth Pike is against restricted approaches to linguistics and chooses to start in linguistic analysis from social interaction which opens perspectives for studying dialogue, sentence, pronunciation, differences between people in particular and various contexts.

Tagmemics theory is complex, because it requires considering context 'at every step: that is, in all perception and experience and knowledge'. This theory is synonymous to *unit-in-context*.

We may approach things that have some kind of relationship in so many different ways, and while trying to determine the nature of the relationships between them, we tend to look for what is useful, but 'so often, [we are obliged to do so] on the form in which facts are given'.

Pike wants his theory to be suitable to as many fields and situations as possible and not only to linguistics. He states, 'Human emic experience is also the target, not merely linguistics'. The Tagmemics theory came as a result of so many researches and attempts to find as general principles that would be applicable to a wide range of languages. The theory revealed itself to be even applicable to other fields of research, such as anthropology.

A **Tagmeme** is defined as "The unit comprising a function, for example, a subject and a class of items fulfilling that function (e.g., nouns). It is most suitable in describing languages such as the Central and South American languages to which it has mostly been applied and in which a number of different classes can fulfil the same function or in which the same class can fulfil many functions. Tagmemics is also known as String Constituent Analysis and differs, in part, from Bloomfieldian linguistics in that semantic as well as syntactic function is used in identifying tagmemes. Pike later applied tagmemics to matrix of field theory and English rhetoric.

In addition to his work in tagmemics, Pike has done research in phonology and is the author of *Intonation of American English* (1945); co-edited *Tone Systems of Tibeto-Burman Languages of Nepal, Parts I–IV* (1970); and co-authored *Grammatical Analysis* (1977) and *Songs of Fun and Faith* (1977). Selections from his work were published in *Selected Writings* in 1972.

Kenneth Pike died in 2000 in Dallas (Texas).

<u>Summarizing</u>:

For the Pike school theorizing about language is subordinated to a much more urgent task i.e. the practical analysis of unfamiliar languages for the practical goal of evangelizing the "heathen" nations i.e. non-Christians!

GRICE (1913-1988)

Implicatures

Austin's Oxford colleague H.P. Grice (1913–1988) developed a sophisticated theory of how **Nonliteral aspects of meaning** are generated and recovered through the exploitation of general principles of rational cooperation as adapted to conversational contexts. An utterance such as "she got married and raised a family", for example, would ordinarily convey that she got married before she raised a family. But this "**implicature**," as Grice called it, is not part of the literal meaning of the utterance ("what is said"). It is inferred by the hearer on the basis of his knowledge of what is said and his presumption that the speaker is observing a set of conversational maxims, one of which prescribes that events be mentioned in the temporal order in which they occurred.

The largest and most important class of implicatures consists of those that are generated not by observing the maxims but by openly and obviously violating them. For example, if the author of a letter ostensibly recommending an applicant for a job says only that "Mr. Jones is very punctual and his penmanship is excellent," he thereby flouts the maxim enjoining the speaker (or author) to be as informative as necessary; he may also flout the maxim enjoining relevance. Since both the author and the reader know that more information is wanted and that the author could have provided it, the author implicates that he is prevented from doing so by other considerations, such as politeness. Additionally, therefore, he implicates that the applicant is not qualified for the job.

Metaphor and other figures

Related studies in pragmatics concern the nature of **metaphor** and other figurative language. Indeed, metaphor is of particular interest to philosophers, since its relation to literal meaning is quite problematic. Some philosophers and linguists have held that all speech is at bottom metaphorical. Friedrich Nietzsche (1844–1900), for example, claimed that "literal" truths are simply metaphors that have become worn out and drained of sensuous force. Furthermore, according to this view, metaphor is not merely the classification of familiar things under novel concepts. It is a reflection of the way human beings directly engage their world, the result of a bare human propensity to see some things as naturally grouped with others or as usefully conceived in comparison with others. It is most importantly not a product of reason or calculation, conscious or otherwise. Evidently, this idea bears strong affinities to Wittgenstein's work on rule following.

Figurative language is crucial to the communication of states of mind other than straightforward belief, as well as to the performance of speech acts other than assertion. Poetry, for example, conveys moods and emotions, and moral language is used more often to cajole or prescribe, or to express esteem or disdain, than simply to state one's ethical beliefs. (E.B.)

<u>Summarising:</u>
Linguists and philosophers such as Grice stressed the important fact that "meaning" could only be attained if we focus on "communication," as it is the link between speaker and hearer(s). British American philosopher

Herbert Paul Grice passed away in 1988.

PEIRCE (1839-1914)

Charles Sanders Peirce, born September 10th 1839, is an American philosopher, logician, mathematician and scientist. He is referred to as "the father of **pragmatism**." He had somewhat a special character.

He was first a student of chemistry, and then was employed as a scientist for 30 years. He then moved his intellectual interest to philosophy and made an important impact on the **logical** studies of his time. Logic for him is much wider than is usually considered. It includes the usual topics, to which he adds **epistemology** and the philosophy of science. For him logic is deeply rooted in the science of signs (semiotics).

In fact, **Semiotics** is usually linked to his name as its founder, the same as **Semiologie** is linked to Saussure's name in Europe. This was in the midst of the big row of the 20th century between defenders of **logical positivism** and **philosophers of language** (see Wittgenstein). He refined the major concepts of deductive, mathematical and adductive reasoning.

Ever since the year 1886, Peirce saw the possibility of linking **logical operation** to **electrical circuits**, thus opening the door for hardware **computer** buildings. Paul Weiss described Charles Peirce as : "the most original and versatile of American philosophers and America's greatest logician."

He is further considered as a **realistic thinker**. Concerning the concept of "**modality**" he wrote: "I formerly defined the possible as that which in a given state of information (real or feign) we do not know not to be true. But this definition today seems to me only a twisted phrase which, by means of two negatives, conceals an **anacoluthon**. We know in advance of experience that certain things are not true, because we see they are impossible" (1868).

He still kept certain previous definitions of logic (information states), but stressed the need for the science of pragmatics to be deeply rooted in the "real modality" for things to be conceived under different circumstances.

As a staunch believer in **God**, Peirce conceived religion as a deep instinct that can be experienced over ideas, facts and habits. In his <u>A Neglected Argument for the Reality of God</u> (1908) Peirce suggests the urgent of God as "necessary being" (by opposition of man "potential or conditional being"). God transcends human ideas, facts and habits, including scientific progress. (see the Great Debate at University of Washington 1995)

The hypothesis supposing an "infinitely incomprehensible" being, disregard its tremendous size, it is:
a) defined without limit,
b) it is vague and true at the same time, and
c) Peirce believes in human **free will** and in some kind of human **immortality**.

Summarizing:
For Peirce, like for other ordinary language philosophers, language is a tool for communication, which has its own logic, and hence must be approached from this angle.

Charles Sanders Peirce passed away April 19th 1914.

[Not to confuse with Franklin Peirce 1804-1869]

CONCLUSION

Usually, people equate American linguistics with Chomsky's Transformational -Generative Grammar (1957). As a matter of fact there are, at least three main dominant movements of language study in the USA, side by side, with (or vs.) Chomsky's, those are William Labov's Sociolinguistics, and Kenneth Pike's Tagmemics.

William Labov is concerned with "the language spoken in New York City": how you can determine the identity, and the social class of the speaker from his speech (see Higgins) and most interestingly from his use of the [r] sound or lack of use of this liquid (**retroflex**).

As for Pike and his school, they are very successful translators of the Holy Bible into all the languages and dialects of the world so as to transmit the divine message to every person in his own mother tongue. "No one has any excuse on the day of judgement."

Finally, Chomsky's TG (to which I belong) investigates the nature of language, it considers the simple (or complex) sentence as the unit of language, as the sentence is the one constituent that can express an idea, and is the basis for analytic truth.

While the first trend seeks the social classes, the second the message of Christ, the third focuses on the nature of language; its phonetic, syntactic and semantic components, dealt with in the light of a Universal Grammar.

Chomsky's grammar is closer to Arabic than the others, as it is based on rational analogy and linguistic universals. It reminds us of the dichotomies we find in

Sibawaihi's work. Generativists are concerned with the native speaker's competence as Sibawayh refers continually to "those, whose Arabic is reliable." Lately, Chomsky recognized the "suggestive" character of the Arabic language.
(see Chomsky 1997)

Some linguists focused on the word (Bloomfield), others on discourse (Harris) while the generativists focused on the sentence, which is between the two trends, as the word remains "ambiguous" as long as it is not predicated.

Discourse i.e. talks, books, ideologies, even religions can be summed up in one sentence. Buddhism can be summed up in: 'be patient', Hinduism: 'everything has a soul', Judaism: 'God chose his people', Christianity: 'the Messiah is the Saviour,' Islam: 'God is one.'

Discourse can be either spoken or written, as mentioned before. Spoken discourse is alive and is better dealt with, as it is surrounded by a number of pragmatic indices that determine the meaning of the speaker's message and his intention. Still this is often a treasure with a lost key.

Robert Le Page believes that the research in discourse and language use is more difficult than the analysis of 'money use'. The latter has so far defeated all attempts made by the economists. In addition to the text and the pragmatics elements, you may need to know the whole human experience.

[Discourse [context [human experience]]]

While generativists search in the structure of the sentence (infinite number) and its analytic (internal) truth, literary people of novel, drama and poetry search the message and the aesthetic features of the text.

The message of the literary text can be summed up in one simple sentence, as said before, whereas aesthetics, and ecstasy cannot be scientifically quantified. (see Jacobson's poetics)

ANOTHER way of looking at American Linguistics is to divide it into three trends: "Bloomfieldians," "Chomskyans" and "Cognitivists." In fact, American Linguistics started much earlier than these. The history of linguistics in the United States began so as to achieve a greater understanding of humans and their languages. By trying to find a greater 'parent language' through similarities in different languages, a number of connections were discovered.

William Dwight **Whitney**, the first US taught academic linguist, founded the American philological association in 1869. During his professional career, he served as president of the Invention of American Philologists. He was also the first editor-in-chief of the English Century Dictionary, 1889-1891.

The "American Saussure" however is Franz Boas with his famous Handbook of American Indian Languages, in which he defended his relativist concept, against nationalistic ideologies of Europe of the 30s. According to him, Language, race and culture are to be separated.

Linguistics in the 1920s had focused on grammatical analyses and grammatical structure, especially of languages indigenous to North America, such as Chippewa, Apache, and many others. In recent years, the study of

Linguistics in the United States has broadened its scope to include non-standard varieties of English, as well as the question of whether language perpetuates social inequalities.

Then, came towering Leonard Bloomfield, who defended mechanistic discovery procedures and the behaviourist psychology. He dealt mainly with phonology and morphology, and rejected semantics as unscientific. The other famous linguists who were active in the first half of the 20th century included Edward Sapir, Benjamin Whorf and Charles Hockett (item & arrangement, item & process, and portmanteau). Then came pure structuralists such as Zellig Harris and missionary linguists such as Kenneth Pike.

From the 1950s, American linguistic tradition began to diverge from the European (Saussurean) structuralism, notably with Noam Chomsky's "nativism" and "transformational" grammar. Chomsky is often described as the "father of modern Linguistics". His model kept evolving (diverging?) to give rise to a wide variety of competing grammatical frameworks, ending with the well-known "Linguistics wars" of the 1970s.

Besides Chomsky's school, with its "Linguistics wars", you find the American Functional School led by Talmy Givon, and Cognitive Grammar advocated by Ronald Langacker and others. John McWhortter, represents the American School specialising in Afro-American studies, and Linguistic Typology and Universals, led by Joseph Greenberg.

APPENDICES

Aim
The American Indian Movement is a Native American grassroots movement founded in July 1968 in Minneapolis, Minnesota, initially centered in urban areas to address systemic issues of poverty, discrimination, and police brutality against Native Americans.

Arabic
Arabic is a Semitic language (together with Hebrew and Aramaic). Bernard Comrie of California university, states: "the Arabic language is already studied intensively as the language of a major culture and of a major religion; here I want to adopt a narrower perspective, to show even those linguists who do not, or do not yet, share such broader cultural perspective on Arabic

studies that the Arabic language has much to offer them." (Comrie, 1990). Chomsky states: "note also that a language might allow both weak and strong Inflection, hence weak and strong NP-features: Arabic is a suggestive case, with SVO versus VSO correlating with the richness of visible verb inflection" (*Minimalist Program* 1997).

Aristotle

[Chomsky has been called the New Aristotle]

"Language" is defined as speech sounds built to convey meaning.

If we listened to the geniuses of the past, such as Aristotle, "what do they say about "language?"

Aristotle was the tutor of Alexander the great. He was born in

Macedonia in the year 384 BC and together with Plato is one of the greatest philosophers of all times. He was a true academic; he dealt with physics, astronomy, rhetoric, literature, political sciences and history. His principles are considered as the premises of modern scientific thought.

He was a philosopher, but philosophy, in his time, meant all fields of knowledge. It was referred to as wisdom. He was renown for his logic essentially by setting its foundations in his book known as the *Organon*. This helped him in organizing the way of correct thought so as to answer the sophists who were diverting from correct thinking. They could defend the thing and its opposite and deny reality as well as the abstract, and the spiritual including the existence of God. They also defended the dogma of creation by accident.

To answer "accident" Aristotle used his syllogism:

-All moving need a mover

-The world is moving

-The world has a mover

The chariot moves by a horse, man moves by his will, the wind moves the air. We notice that the world is moving: the night then the day, the cycle of the seasons, the tide of the sea, the running of the rivers and the moving of the stars. They must have a mover.

The mover is **God**.

Eskimo-Aleut languages
Eskimo-Aleut languages are the languages spoken in Greenland, Canada and Alaska, together with eastern Siberia, by Eskimo and Aleut people. Aleut survived only,

together with many dialects. Eskimo includes Inuits and Yupik, with mutually unintelligible dialects. The term Aleut is usually used on the other side of the Bering Strait, by the Russians.

Generative Morphology
Generative grammar is interested in providing a precise and explicit characterization of "what it is that you know when you know a language?" The same thing holds true for the domain of morphology.

Morphology deals with word structure and word formation. It is the part of that knowledge of language which linguists regard as properly linguistic. Thus morphology is something which linguistic theory has to account for, in the same way that it accounts for knowledge of phonological patterns and knowledge of syntactic structures.

From the word morphology, we extract the word morpheme: it is the minimal meaningful unit/element in language, e.g. <u>anti</u> and <u>ism</u> tend to be used like words, and probably are words (in addition of being morphemes). The word, <u>establish</u> is also a morpheme (in addition of being a word) what unites all these entities is that:

(i) they seem to contribute some sort of meaning or at least function, to the word of which they are a compound and,

(ii) (ii) they can themselves be decomposed into smaller morphemes.

It is useful to distinguish those morphemes which are also words in their own right from those which only appear as a proper subpart of a word. The forms are called free morphemes and the latter bound morphemes (see Bloomfield 1933)

Types of Morphemes

Root: is the irreducible core of a word, with absolutely nothing else attached to it. It is the part that is always present, possibly with some modification.

Infix
It is an affix inserted into the root itself. Infixes are very common in Semitic languages like Arabic and Hebrew. Infixes are rare in English.

Stem
It is that part of the word that is in existence before any inflectional affixes have been added. Consider the examples below:

Noun	Plural
cat	-s
worker	-s

In the word form cats, the plural inflectional suffix –s is attached to the simple stem cat, which is a bare root. In workers the same.

Typically, a morphologically complex (or polymorph) word will contain a central morpheme, which contributes the basic meaning, and collection of other morphemes serving to notify this meaning in various ways. Consider the word <u>disagreements</u> in English, we dissect a basic morpheme which is <u>agree</u> and three bound morphemes which are <u>dis</u>-, -<u>ment</u> and -<u>s</u>. We call <u>agree</u> the root and the other (bound) morphemes) affixes. <u>Dis</u>- which comes to the left of the root is a prefix, while the morphemes –<u>ment</u> and –<u>s</u> which come to the right are suffixes. The whole word <u>disagreements</u>, is called a **stem**.

One of the facts about morphemes in linguistics theory is that they leave a physical (i.e. phonetic and phonological) form and also a meaning or function within the grammatical system. Consider the plural endings in the words below:

(1)
Cats
Dogs
Horses

The regular plural ending (which is regarded as a morpheme) is realized in three different pronunciations /s/ /z/ and /iz/, since these three elements all represent a morpheme they are called morphs. These are the realizations (i.e. alternative forms) of a single morpheme which we can represent as -z. we say that the morphs /s/, /z/, /iz/ are allomorphs of –z and that the plural morpheme exhibits allomorphy. The allomorphy in (1) is conditioned entirely by phonology. By this I mean that the choice of the allomorph for the plural suffix depends solely on the pronunciation of the stem.

(Allomorphy, e.g. good better best, go went , park-ed, miss-ed, clean-ed. It should be observed that the morpheme (-ed) is realized in three different shapes depending on the nature of the last consonant of the base).

By morphological operation, we mean the different ways in which the phological form of words are obtained.

Traditional grammarians usually distinguished between two main types of morphological operations: **inflectional** (i.e. boys), and **Derivation** (change the meaning of the base e.g. kind → un-kind-ly)

Generative Phonology
The 'Phoneme' was the target of the American Descriptivists. By all

means "discovery procedures' were made to decipher this meaningful 'atom' of language from the continuum stretch of sounds of alien (usually Native American) languages, under study. 'For Chomsky, on the other hand, it might well be claimed that syntax is the heart of linguistic science.' (see Samson 1980). Still Chomsky states that Phonology is more interesting to study as it is easier to reach conclusions in it than in syntax. Chomsky's grammar defines or rather 'generates' (in the **mathematical** sense) well formed sentences. Generative phonology is the creation of Morris Halle of MIT, himself a student of **Jakobson**.

Bloomfield, and many of his co-workers believed that the 'phoneme' was the ultimate unit in the building of language. Rather, the new approach is based on the 'distinctive parameter bundles'. We do indeed find many examples of alternations that affects 'natural classes' of sounds rather than single ones. So phonology must be dealt with in terms of phonetic features rather than in terms of unitary segments.

The pair 'Obstruants/sonorant' stands for the sounds, interrupting the air flow and those permitting the free air way. Both behave as a natural class. Final voiced obstruants are devoiced e.g. German word final [d] becomes [t] as in [Bad] pronounced [bat], as well as the rest [b], [d], [g] becoming [p], [t] and [k] respectively. Therefore, the phonological information must be dealt with in terms of Binary-**Distinctive-features**. (see Jakobson)

This approach applies neatly across languages. Samson states "distinctive features might have more direct meaning in acoustic than in articulatory terms (…). In any case, even if the acoustic or perceptual effect of labialization were similar or even identical to that of pharygalization, say, nevertheless a complete description of Arabic would have to state that speakers use the latter rather than the former articulation, and vice versa in Twi." (see Sampson 1980)

Generative Semantics
Generative semantics is a trend of thought advanced within generative grammar, by George Lakoff, James McCawley, Paul Postal, Haj Ross, and others that considers the deep structure of a sentence as the semantic component, from which the surface (PF) can be derived.

Their analysis starts by giving the sentence its proper semantic representation; you state the conditions of derivation and then move to the generation of the surface structure i.e. the real actual utterance. There is no intermediate level between semantic representation and final output of the transformational operation, i.e. surface structure.

This goes indeed against Chomsky's (**EST**) hypothesis, which consists of saying that you need two deep structures, so to speak, before you try and reach the surface structure. Three levels for Chomsky: semantic, deep and surface structures, semantic and surface structures for the Generative semanticists. And, hence the "Linguistics Wars" that ensued (see Newmeyer 1980).

The term 'generative' is more constrained in this theory.

Generative Syntax

Syntax is another sub-branch of Linguistics which deals with how words are combined into sentences (vs. morphology).

Word classes (parts of speech) are very important in a syntactic analysis: nouns, verbs, adjectives, adverbs. e.g.

<u>The teachers fear the strength of the blackbirds</u>

The words <u>teachers</u>, <u>strength</u> and <u>blackbirds</u> are nouns. Each noun is accompanied by a determiner, something which helps to identify what is being referred to.

Other determiners are indefinite articles (<u>a, an</u>), possessive adjectives (<u>my</u>) numerals (<u>three</u>) and so on.

The word <u>fear</u> is a verb, a class that has the functions of indicating an action or a state of being.

<u>Of</u> is a preposition, a class that indicates a relationship between other elements of the utterance.

Having identified the words in such sentence in terms of their appropriate classes, we can represent the sentence S as follows:

S> art, N, V, Art, N, prep, art, N

Other classes are the pronoun, the adjective, the adverb and the conjunction.

A pronoun replaces a noun and anything that may accompany it; thus the pronoun <u>they</u> could be substituted for <u>the teachers</u> and the pronoun <u>them</u> could be substituted for <u>the blackbirds</u>.

An adjective provides more information about the thing or person indicated by the noun. The adjective <u>old</u> may be inserted between <u>the</u> and <u>teachers</u>.

   The very old teachers greatly fear the blackbirds

We have two adverbs: <u>very</u> which is qualifying an adjective and <u>greatly</u> which is qualifying the verb.

Adding <u>and</u> to <u>the blackbirds</u> sequence we are using a conjunction, a word which links the elements of the utterance.

The sequence <u>the very old teachers</u> is acceptable in English. The sequence <u>old the very teachers</u> is not. Using the word classes, we can devise rules to define what is grammatically acceptable and what is not.

In English, the order art, adv, adj, is acceptable; whereas the order adj, art, adv, N is not.

Thus the rules which govern the structure of utterances are known as Phrase Structure Rules. The function of such rules in a language such as English is to allow for the generation of grammatical sentences. This being the case, they constitute a generative grammar for that language.

The (constituent) structure of the sentence, <u>the very old teachers greatly fear the blackbirds</u> can be described as follows:

S> art, adv, adj, N, adv, V, art, N

This description, however, shows simply that the sentence is linear and fails to capture the fact that it has a more complex, hierarchical structure.

Thus, the four words <u>the very old teachers</u> have a coherent reference, whereas the four words <u>very old teachers greatly</u> do not.

The coherence of the sequence <u>the very old teachers</u> allows it to constitute a phrase. In this example, we have a noun phrase, the key word or head being a noun (i.e. <u>teachers</u>)

The utterance <u>the very old teachers</u> is a subject and the other part of the sentence <u>greatly fear the blackbirds</u> is called its predicate. Similarly, one can use the terms topic and comment and the terms theme and rheme.

A sequence with a subject and a predicate constitutes a clause. This latter may be a whole sentence, or part of it.

It may consist of more than one clause, as in [many people think] [that the teachers greatly fear the blackbirds]. The second clause (that is underlined) is known as a dependent or subordinate clause.

A linguist will analyse the sentence: The very old teachers greatly fear the blackbirds as a noun phrase and a verb phrase.

In linguistic notation: S, NP, VP. This represents a deeper level of analysis than:

S>art,adv,adj,N,adv,V,art,N.

Analysis at this deeper level allows one to define more general principles of sentence structure. On this basis, a noun phrase precedes a verb phrase in a declarative sentence, whether that noun is the very old teachers or simply they.

There are two levels of analysis that can be related to each other by constructing a tree diagram as shown below:

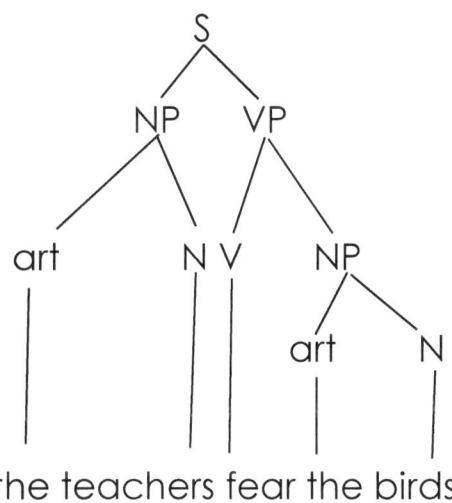

the teachers fear the birds

The very old teachers greatly fear the blackbirds
[art adv adj N adv V art N] (simplified)

Suppose you want to specify <u>the blackbirds</u> concerned by adding to it <u>in the park</u> in which case it is a prepositional phrase.

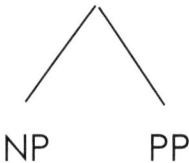

NP   PP

[The black birds] [in the park]

It should be observed that the elements on one level are constituents of those on a higher lever, or immediate constituents of those on the level immediately above.

Words are immediate constituents of a phrase as <u>the teachers</u> in: <u>the teachers died</u>. There may be more than one phrase and clauses between word and sentence.

To understand the grammar of a language, one needs to know what can serve as constituents of an element. One needs to know also that a noun phrase must contain a noun or a pronoun.

Our awareness of what is and what is not a well-formed utterance helps us to understand almost immediately the meaning of a sentence and to disregard false interpretation.
(Bellouchi)

Formal Linguistics
It is the study of grammar of the development of theories as to how language works and is organized. Formal linguistics compares grammars of different languages, and by identifying and studying the elements common among them, seeks to discover the most efficient way to describe language in general. The ultimate goal is "Universal Grammar" –the development of a theory to explain how the human brain processes language. Within formal linguistics, there are three main schools of thought: traditional, structural and transformational.

Traditional grammar is the one that is most familiar to the majority of us. A typical definition in traditional grammar is 'a noun is a person, place, or thing.' 'adjective clause', noun clause', 'complements', etc. Structural linguistics was a principally American phenomenon of the 1940's. in linguistics, it was principally concerned with phonology, morphology and syntax. Transformational-generative approach to the description of language was introduced in 1957 by Chomsky.

Gengo Kenkyu
[言語研究**]**（Chomsky's latest publication, 2021）

The questions posed have many aspects. I would like to begin with some general remarks on the nature of the inquiry, and then turn to the kinds of problems that arise and what might constitute authentic answers to them. The next step is an effort at principled reconstruction of the basic ideas, followed by extension to new empirical domains, and then a few final reflections.

The Nature of the Inquiry: It is useful, I think, to reflect a little on the general background of our inquiry before turning to the specific details of the problems at hand. In particular, to place in a more general context the nature and development of the generative enterprise that began to develop in mid-20th century — guiding concerns that are, not surprisingly, becoming clearer as the enterprise is pursued and surely with surprises to come. I think it may be entering a new phase, one with severe challenges and exciting prospects.

From infancy, children are trying **to make sense of the puzzling world** around them, and a similar quest is a constant theme of cultural history in all societies we know of. In the modern world, there have been periods where willingness to be puzzled about the world became the spirit of the age, leading to what are sometimes called "scientific revolutions." One such period was the 17th century. Alfred North Whitehead hardly exaggerated when he wrote that ever since, our "intellectual life … has been living upon the accumulated capital of ideas provided for them by the genius of the seventeenth century." (Chomsky, PC)

Hebrew
"During the later Middle Ages Arabic and Hebrew had been studied in Europe, and in the University of Paris in the fourteenth century both languages were officially recognized. Roger Bacon wrote a grammar of Hebrew and knew Arabic. Indeed the necessity

of some knowledge of Hebrew, as the language of the Old Testament, had been realized sporadically since the time of Jerome (345-420); but such studies had often been undertaken in a clandestine, half shamefaced manner, Christians fearing charges of associating with the enemies of the church and Jews fearing the accusation of **proselytizing**. Its biblical status had given Hebrew a place alongside Latin and Greek as a language worthy of attention. Isadore (seventh century) along with many others regarded it as the language of God and therefore the first language to be spoken on earth." (see Robins 1967)

Hermann, Hirt (1865- 1936)
"German linguist whose comprehensive *Indogermanische Grammatik* (1921; "Indo-European Grammar"), remains influential. Earlier, Hirt had made original studies of accent and Umlaut

(vowel changes) in Indo-European. His concern with prehistory extended beyond language to the Indo-European people and their culture, which he treated in *Die Indogermanen,* (1905; "The Indo-Europeans"). The major part of his professional life was spent as professor of Indo-European philology and Sanskrit at the University of Giessen (1912–36). (E. B.)

Inuit language
Inuit means "the people" (man). Those are the Eskimo languages spoken in the north east areas including Alaska, Canada and Greenland. There is a dialectal continuum, which makes many of these dialects mutually intelligible.

Kwakiutl
Northwest pacific coast, notably British Columbia, Vancouver,

languages: Haisla, Heiltsuq, and southern Kwakiutl. The Kwakiutl Indians are related to their (neighbors?) Nootka.

Language centrism

It is noteworthy that each nation boasts of having being given the best language on earth. Chomsky states: "Diderot concludes that French is unique among languages in the degree to which the order of words corresponds to the natural order of thoughts and ideas (Diderot, 1751. Thus 'Quel que soit l'ordre des termes dans une langue ancienne ou moderne, l'esprit de l'écrivain a suivi l'ordre didactique de la langue française' (); 'nous disons les choses en français, comme l'esprit est forcé de les considérer en quelque langue qu'on écrive'(). with admirable consistency he goes on to conclude that 'notre langue pédestre a sur les autres l'avantage de l'utile sur l'agréable'" (see Chomsky 1965)

Menominee
North American Indians living between Wisconsin and Michigan, first reported by missionary Jean Nicolet (1639). They lived on wild rice, corn, beans, tobacco, fishing and hunting. They sold their rights to the US government. Their reservation came to an end in 1961, and became a county of Wisconsin. Agitation happened from time to time, with some animosity towards the white man.

Minimalism
Finally, Chomsky moved further from 'syntactic transformations' to morphological considerations. He states: "note also that a language might allow both weak and strong Inflection, hence weak and string NP-features." (see Chomsky 1997).

The TG theory lately turned more morphological than syntactic, more typology than universal and more appropriate to language such Hebrew and Arabic.

Minimalist guidelines:
A) A linguistic expression is a pair (a, b) generated by the minimal deviation satisfying interface conditions
B) The interface levels are the only levels of linguistic representation (PF/LF)
C) All conditions concern the interface
D) Derivations concerned are driven by morphological properties (attract/move)
E) Economy is expressed in terms of greed and procrastinate (Chomsky 1997)

Navaho

the Navaho are the most populous of all Indian groups in the United States, with about 170,000 individuals in the late 20th most other Athabascan-speaking Indians still live, but it was probably between AD 900 and 1200. Those early Navajo would have borne more resemblance to contemporary Apache than to contemporary Navajo, because the Navajo came under the strong influence of the Pueblo Indians. These Pueblo influences included farming as the primary mode of subsistence, with a concomitant trend toward a sedentary existence. In historical times, farming has been supplemented—and, in some regions, superseded—by herding of sheep, goats, and cattle.

The Navajo resemble other Apachean peoples in their lack of a centralized tribal or political organization. Formerly, they were organized into small bands of related kinsmen, with local headmen. Similar groups, based on locality of residence rather than kinship, still exist, and many of these local groups have elected headmen. A Navajo local group is not a village or town but rather a collection of dwellings scattered over a wide area. (E. B.)

Saussure (1857-1913)

"What is language?"
To answer this anthological question, the answers were many. In the 19th c. there was a fashion that wanted to equate "language" studies with biology; being influenced by Darwinian ideology. It was the case of German philologists such as Paul and Schlecher. Language was given the biological analogy of species such as "carrots" or "cats".

The man who broke with the Darwinian paradigm was Saussure. For him language is a "social fact" rather than a biological tangible thing. He was influenced by Emil Durkheim notion of "collective mind."

His full name Mongin Ferdinand de Saussure was born in Geneva in 1857, from a Huguenot family that had to flee the civil wars in France 16th c. his book *Cours de Linguistique Générale* (1916) posthumous is considered as the starting point of modern linguistics and himself as the father of synchronic linguistics. (a genius!)

For him the proper study of language should see "language" as a system at one given point in time (disregarding any historical dimension). It is similar to the game of chess, as no history is relevant in that sports.

Although Saussure himself worked as a student in the historical approach for the reconstruction of indo-European languages, and even taught in the same frame, he managed to see the relevance of the other approach. For the language user it is irrelevant to known about the evolution of the English language from the time of Shakespeare, let alone Chaucer (that was closer to German than to modern English!)

All the speaker of English needs to know is how to use it NOW. He can ignore its past or even its structure. All he has to do is to be able to use it in accordance of what is intelligible to the people in London, Oxford Street (or any other speech area for that matter). No oddities!

Saussure is famous for his dichotomies: synchronic vs. diachronic, langue vs. parole, signifié vs. significant", paradigmatic vs. sytagmatic. Language is form (-imec) non-substance (-itic). That is a meaningful sign rather than a sound or a piece of ink on a paper or chalk on the blackboard! (see Khalid Touzani's soldier's story)

If language is a structure, it should be studied as a structure. Hence the name of the method, (or ideology?) known as Structuralism. What does that mean? It means that each item (word or morpheme) of the system has no intrinsic value but rather derives its value from its relations with the other items. It's a brick in the wall! By itself it has no meaning; no (intrinsic) value.

Saussure was influenced by French Emil Durkehime,'s notion of the "collective mind" or German Volkgeist, language stands in contrast with biological, physical, or even psychological facts (vs.

Chomsky). It is an abstract but socially effective fact like "stones" ("Hit one with your dagger and sword but not with your word!"). It can be exemplified by English Mister Maddox coming to the university to teach wearing a skirt. No way! His neighboring Scotsmen would put on the kilt without fear nor shame. So, similarly language has got its own social impact. (see Sampson 1980)

What is language? "**Language is an arbitrary sign system.**"

Sibawaihi (760-793)

(See Chomsky's connections)

Sibawayh is the most famous Arabic grammarian. After studying in Basra, Iraq, with prominent grammarians, Sibawayh received recognition as a great grammarian himself. Sibawayh is said to have left Iraq and retired to Shiraz after losing a debate with a rival on Bedouin Arabic usage, to die at a very young age (33 years). His left us though a monumental work on Arabic i.e. *al-Kitab* ("The Book"). This famous work of his was frequently used by later scholars, including Noam Chomsky. (see Ben Rochd 2020)

Speech Acts Theory

After Austin's death in 1960, Speech Act Theory was deepened and refined by his American student **John R. Searle**. In *The Construction of Social Reality* (1995), Searle argued that many social and political institutions are created through speech acts. Money, for example, is created through a declaration by a government to the effect that pieces of paper or metal of a certain manufacture and design are to count as money. Many institutions, such as banks, universities, and police departments, are social entities created through similar speech acts. Searle's development of speech act theory was thus an unexpected extension of the philosophy of language into social and political theory. (E. B.)

GLOSSARY

Affix
An inflectional or derivational element added to a base to form a (word) stem, e.g. –ed added to jump to give jumped.

Algorithm
A computing term referring to program, use as a solution to a problem.

American English
Sometimes referred to as GA (General American) by contrast with RP (British English). "The differences between RP and GA concern spelling, vocabulary and pronunciation e.g. center vs centre, garbage for rubbish, and water /wodə/.
(see Ben Rochd 2021c)

Analogy
The process to create new words from the pattern of previous ones. Arabic Verb Analogy is famous. It is also a specific characteristic of child language.

Analytic
Analytic truth depends on the internal structure of the sentence, by opposition to synthetic truth depending on empirical facts.

Anaphoric
Such as reflexives, having to do with (co)reference e.g. he likes <u>himself</u>.

Anthropology
The science that studies **man**; his physiology, anatomy, sociology, family, beliefs, and culture.

Antonymy
Opposite in meaning e.g. bad boys v good boys.

Argument
In logic denoting an element which is part of a relationship such as 5> 4 "greater than."

Articulators
The parts of the speech tract that come together to produce speech sounds e.g. the two lips.

Ashkenazi
Jews of Germany and Eastern Europe vs. Sephardic Jews of the Middle East.

Base
The bare part of the word, before any affixation takes place.

Behaviourism
A school of psychology, that relies on the external observation of human conduct, considering it as the only scientific approach available.

Catharsis
The purification of the soul through purity or fear as in tragedy.

Case
A grammatical category that indicates the grammatical function of nouns and verbs (in Arabic), by inflections affecting the ending of the words.

Chippewa
American Indian language, of the Big Lakes.

Cognitive
Cognitive (vs. denotative) meaning is the original 'neutral' meaning of the words by opposition to their denotative meaning e.g. <u>popular</u>.

Deictic
Reference depending on the context, or situation e.g. there.

Derivation
A morphological term designating the operation consisting of adding affixes to the stem so as to yield new words e.g. happy →happiness.

Determinism
A philosophy that advocates that everything is pre-determined by God, (nature, history, or language) and that human choice and freedom is an illusion.

Diglossia
Two forms of a given language; one considered as high and one as low.

Distinctive features
A Chomsky & Halle's terminology referring to the characteristics of a sound, that makes a class vs. phoneme.

English
The official language of England, USA, and the commonwealth. It is classified as a Germanic language.

Entailment
The logical result of the analysis of the meaning of a sentence e.g. John killed Mary → Mary died.

Ethnology
Part of anthropology, dealing with the differences and similarities of different cultures.

Free Form
Bloomfieldian term to refer to the stem of a word vs. bound form, which cannot occur alone.

Generative grammar
The finite set of rules, which produces an infinite set of sentences.

German
Official language of Germany, Austria and part of Switzerland. The prototype of the Germanic languages; including English.

Head
The principle part of a constituent such as verb for verb phrase, etc.

Hyponymy
Higher in specificity of a term e.g. tulip for flower.

ICA (Immediate constituent analysis)
the Bloomfieldian syntactic approach, which proceeds from the highest constituent (the sentence) to the lowest (the phoneme).

Icon
Initially a representation of **Christ**, then a perfect representative symbol for something.

Idiolect
The speech characteristic to one single individual.

Illocution
A term used in Speech Acts Theory, referring to the speaker's act of speaking. (see **Searl**)

Inflection
A word ending to mark its syntactic function, as in past work + -ed.

Inuit
Eskimo tribes of north American and Greenland [*inuk*: a man].

IPA
International Phonetic Alphabet

Item & arrangement
A morphological approach, seeing words as a sequence of morphemes e.g. the+boy+hit+the+ball.

Item & process
A morphological approach, seeing words as derived from other items e.g. take → took, involved a vowel transformation.

Jones (1746-1794)
Sir William Jones (1746-1794) was the first European Sanskrit scholar. This led to comparative studies focusing on the language change in **Indo-European** language family e.g. *mata* mother, *dvatu* two. It became the fashion of 19th c. European Linguistics

Kawkiutl
Canadian Indian language (British Columbia).

Lamb (1929-)
Sidney Lamb is an American linguist and follower of Hjelmslev's Copenhagen school.

Lexical item
A word with independent (complete) meaning.

Liquid
A frictionless sound with partial obstruction of the air stream e.g. (l), (r).

Locution
In the speech acts theory, it refers to the act of performing a meaningful utterance.

Logical constant
A fixed item combining with variables in logical calculus e.g. & (and), V (or), etc.

Mechanistic
In philosophy, the mechanism theory i.e. a system (structure) the parts of which perform together a given function, like a machine.

Metathesis
The transposition of the sounds of a given word.

Modality
A logical term concerned with the probability of certainty of certain events, e.g. may be, certainly, never, etc.

Morpheme
The minimal unit of grammar of a given language.

Ontology
A branch of philosophy concerned with the real existence of things.

Ordering
A term in Chomsky's grammar, refereeing to the order or cycle of application of transformations as in e.g. help yourself, won't you? (see Feeding vs. bleeding, Kayne 1977)

Output conditions
A TG grammar term refereeing to the conditions imposed on the surface structure operating as 'filter' v selectional restrictions imposed on the deep structure.

Panini (5th c. BC)
[Bloomfield recognised his debt to Panini]
Ancient Indian linguist, author of the first Sanskrit grammar.

Parameter
The fixed element of an equation v. variables.

Parsing
The (case) analysis of the constituents of a sentence, such as subject, complement, etc.

Perlocution
In the speech acts theory, it refers to the effect an utterance has on the listener, in his feelings, beliefs, behaviour, i.e. frightening,

degrading, reconciling, sympathizing, etc.

Phoneme
The minimal unit of sound of a given language.

Plosive
A (stop) consonant characterized by an explosion i.e. sudden release of the closure e.g. b.

Portmanteau
A morphological concept, seeing words as consisting of two morphemes e.g. French au = à+le, Afro-American.

Predicate calculus
(see quantification)

Psychic distance
Keeping the "psychic distance" means to try an achieve objectivity vis-à-vis our own person and environment; looking at them from the outside, as it were.

Quantification
The predication affects which part (or whole) of a class e.g. all men are mortal, some men are poets.

Reference
The semantic relation (v. sense) between an expression and the objects or persons it refers to.

Reflexive
A reflexive is used for co-reference of the subject and the object e.g. in the soldiers killed <u>themselves</u>.

Relativism
Having meaning, depending on other factors, as an ideology viz. nothing is absolute.

Root
The part of the word which remains after the deletion of all derivational and inflectional affixes.

Sanskrit
The ancient language of India; considered as the language of the Vedas (the holy Book of the Hindus).

Scope
The range of an operator's application e.g. negation affecting the items included within the brackets e.g. no (bread and water).

Semiotics
The study of signs, with the reference to ideas, or objects in the real world.

Small Potatoes
Some at Berlin University denied any connection between Sibawaih and Chomsky, when he himself confirmed it. (personal communication)

Speech community
A group of people speaking the same language.

Structuralism
Bloomfieldian segmentation and classification of the phonetic and morphological items of language. Ideologically, it is the idea that elements derive their value from their oppositions within the structure. It applies to social sciences, literature and anthropology.

Stylistics
Word (and sentence) meaning determined by 'style' rather than by denotative meaning.

Syllable
A combination of one vowel with one or more consonants.

Synonymy
Words sharing the same meaning e.g. range & choice.

Tagalog
Central Philippines inhabitants, with Philippino as their official language with English. Others are Arebisayan, Cebuano, Hiligaynon, and Salar. They are the languages of some 14 million indigenous.

Tagmemics
Pike argues that linguistic methods are able to identify the functionally important (-emic) features of any aspect of behavior out of the objective (-etic) data.

Takaki
Japanese doctor who treated Beriberi patients.

Talmy Givon
Head of the American Functionalist School.

Transformation
A rule (in Chomsky's grammar) which operates on a structural description, to yield a structural

output e.g. deletion, substitution, addition, e.g. help yourself, won't you?

Typology
The branch of linguistics concerned with the classification of languages, according to some specific structural features e.g. VSO/SVO/VOS, etc.

Umlaut
A phonetic feature, special to some German vowels, as a link between front and back vowels, marked by two dots over e.g. Mann vs. Männer (plural).

Universe of discourse
All the presupposition around a given dialogue, which determines otherwise ambiguous utterances.

Variable
A plus or minus presence of a feature.

Voice
A sound produced by accompanying vibration of the vocal cords e.g. all the vowels and part of the consonant repertoire e.g. b, d, g.

Wundt (1832-1920)
Wilhelm Wundt, is a German psychologist, and a pioneer of experimental psychology.

Yiddish
A language spoken by the Jews of Germany and Eastern Europe. It is a dialect of High German with words from Hebrew, Romance, and Slovenic; and written in the Hebrew alphabet.

Zero
The absence of a feature may be described as "zero." e.g. as in fish (plural).

BIBLIOGRAPHY

Allen J.P.B. & Paul Van Buren. 1975. Chomsky: Selected Readings. OUP, Oxford.
Al Nasir,A. 1985. Sibawaihi, the Phonologist. PhD, York University.
Al Seghayar,M. .1988. On the Syntax of Small Clauses in Arabic. MA, Ottawa University.
Al Waer, M .1981. An Interview with Noam Chomsky. MIT, Cambridge.
Allwood, J.1987. Logic . CUP, Cambridge.
Aitchinson, J. 1985. *Language Change: Progress or Decay*, University Books, NY 1985
Akmaian, A & Heny, F. 1975. Introduction to the principles of transformational syntax. MIT Press.
Aoun, J. 1985. A Grammar of Anaphora. MIT. Cambridge, mass.
Aoun, J. 1986. Generalized Biding. Dordrecht. Foris.
Aitchinson J. 1985. Language Change. Universe Books. NY.

Bach, E. 1974. syntactic Theory. holt Rinehart & Winston.
Bellout, Z.1987. Moroccan Arabic syllabic structure. DES university of Casablanca.
Ben Rochd, E.1982. French Passive. MA, York University.
Ben Rochd, E.1990. Generalized Binding and Pronominalization in Classical Arabic. PhD, UCD.
Ben Rochd, E.1991a. Barriers & Arabic. Linguistica Communicatio 3, 1.
Ben Rochd, E.1991b. "Aoun's Generalized Binding & The Arabic Evidence." Revue Faculté des Lettres, Oujda.
Ben Rochd, E. 1993. Traditional Linguistics. Bawariq, Oujda.
Ben Rochd, E.1994. American Linguistics. Najah, Casablanca.
Ben Rochd, E . 2019. Tradition in Linguistics. Bod. Paris.
Ben Rochd, E. 2020a. Evolution of Chomsky's Transformational Grammar. Bod. Paris.

Ben Rochd, E. 2020b. Words. Bod. Paris.
Ben Rochd, E. 2021a. Sibawaihi's Transformational Grammar. Bod. Paris.
Ben Rochd, E. 2021b. Die Worter. Bod. Paris.
Ben Rochd, E. 2021c. History of Linguistics. Bod. Paris
Ben Rochd, E. 2021d. English. Bod. Paris
Benveniste, E. 1966. Problèmes de linguistique générale. Galimar, Paris.
Bittner, M. & K. Hale. 1993. "Ergativity." MIT, Cambridge.
Bloomfield, L.1933. Language. Holt, New York.
Brumfit & Johnson. 1979. The Communicative Approach To Language Teaching. OUP. Oxford.
Borer, H.1983. Parametric Syntax. Foris, Dordrecht.
Borer, H.1987. "Anaphoric AGR." GLOW, Venice.
Brame, M.1970. Arabic Phonology. PhD MIT.

Busse, W.1974. Klasse Transitivitat Valenz. Fink, Munich.
Carter, M.1968. A Study of Sibawaihi's Principles of Grammatical Analysis. PhD, Oxford.
Chomsky, N.1957. Syntactic Structures. Mouton, The Hague.
Chomsky, N.1965. Aspects of the Theory of Syntax. MIT, Cambridge.
Chomsky, N.1972. Language and Mind. Harcourt, New York.
Chomsky, N.1981. Lectures on Government and Binding. Foris, Dordrecht.
Chomsky, N.1982. Some Concepts and Consequences of the Theory of Government and Binding. MIT, Cambridge.
Chomsky, N.1986. Barriers. MIT, Cambridge.
Chomsky, N.1988. Language and Problems of Knowledge. MIT, Cambridge.
Chomsky, N.1997. Minimalist Program. MIT, Cambridge.

Chomsky, N. & M. Halle. 1968. The Sound Pattern of English. Harper & Row, New York.

Chomsky, N. 2021. Gengo Kenkyu. University of Arizona.

Clark, H. & E. Clark. 1977. Psychology and language. Harcourt. Brace.

Comrie, B. 1991 'On the Importance of Arabic to General Linguistic Theory', in Bernard Comrie and Mushira eid (eds): Perspectives on Arabic Linguistics III, Amsterdam, John Benjamins.

Comrie, B. 1995. Language Universals and Linguistic Typology. Blackwell, Cambridge, USA.

Crystal, D.1985. A Dictionary of Linguistics and Phonetics. Blackwell, Oxford.

Descartes, R. 1974. Discours de la méthode. Les Classiques du Peuple, Paris.

Drimmer, 1968. Black History. Doubleday & CIE. NY.

Emonds, J.1987. "Parts of Speech in Generative Grammar." Linguistic analysis 17, 1-42.
Encyclopedia Britannica.
Fassi-Fehri, A.1982. Lisaniyat wa LuRa 'arabiya. 'uwidat, baris.
Fassi-Fehri, A.1990. "Agreement, Incorporation, Pleonastics, and VSO-SVO order." MIT, Cambridge.
Ferguson, CA. 1959.' Diglossia.' word 15.325-40.
Fromkin, V. & R. Rodman. 1983. An Introduction to Language. Holt-Sanders, New York.
Guamgami, M. 2002, *A Philosophical Approach to English*, ms, Oujda.
Gleason, H.1969. An Introduction to Descriptive Linguistics. Holt-Sanders, New York.
Haegeman, L.1991. Government & Binding Theory. Blackwell, Oxford.
Hale, K.1983. Walpiri and the Grammar of Non-Configurational Languages." Natural language. NLLT 1, 5-47.

Harlow, S. 1995. Evolution of Transformational Grammar. Pergamon. Oxford.
Hoeksema, J.1987. "Logic of Natural Language." Linguistic analysis 11, 155-184.
Jackendoff, R. 1990. Semantic structures. MIT. Cambridge, Mass.
Kayne, R.1975. French Syntax, the Transformational Cycle. MIT, Cambridge.
Kayne, R.1987. "Null Subjects & Clitic Climbing." GLOW, Venice.
King James Version of the Bible.
Koerner, E.F. & R.E. Asher 1995. Concise History of Language Sciences. Pergamon. Cambridge.
Langacker W. R. 1997. Cognitive Grammar. Pergamon. Cambridge.
Le Page, R. 1980. *Acts Of Identity, ms. York University.*
Leech, G. 1974. Semantics. Penguin. Harmondsworth.
Lyons, J. 1970. New Horizons in Linguistics. Penguin. Middlesex.
Lyons, J.1990. Semantics. CUP, Cambridge.

Madkour, I.1969. l'organon dans le monde arabe. J. Vrin, Paris.
Marshall, J.C. 1970. The Biology of Communication in Man and Animals. Penguin. Middlesex.
May, R.1985. Logical Form. MIT, Cambridge.
McCarthy, J.1979. Formal Problems in Semitic Phonology and Morphology. PhD, MIT.
McCarthy, J.1990. Prosodic Morphology & Templatic Morphology. MIT, Cambridge.
Newmeyer, F. 1980. Linguistic theory in America. AP. NY.
O'Connor, J.D. 1966. Better English Pronunciation. CUP. Cambridge.
Palmer, F. 1983. Grammar. Penguin. Middlesex.
Partee, B.1975. "Montague grammar." Linguistic inquiry 6, 203-300.
Pike, K. Lee. 1982. Linguistic Concepts – an Introduction to Tagmemics. University of Nebraska Press, Lincoln & London. A Bison Book.

Radford, A.1981. Transformational Syntax. CUP, Cambridge.
Radford, A.1988. Transformational Grammar. CUP, Cambridge.
Riemsdijk, H & E. Williams. 1986. Theory of Grammar. MIT, Cambridge.
Rizzi, L.1982. Issues in Italian Syntax. Foris, Dordrecht.
Robins, R.H.1967. A Short History of Linguistics. CUP. Cambridge.
Sampson, G. 1980 Schools of Linguistics. Hutchinson. London.
Saussure, F.1977. Course in General Linguistics. Fontana, Oxford.
Schane, S.1973. Generative Phonology. Prentice Hall, New Jersey.
Selkirk, O.1984. Phonology and Syntax. MIT, Cambridge.
Sells, P.1985. Lectures on Cotemporary Syntactic Theories. CSLI, Sanford.
Sibawaih, 1966. al-kitab. Alam al-kitab. Beirut.

Smith N. & D. Wilson. 1980. Modern Linguistics: The Results of Chomsky's Revolution. Penguin Books.

Soams S. & D. Perlmutter. 1997. Syntactic Argumentation and the Structure of English. UCP. LA.

Souaieh, I.1980. Aspects of Arabic Relative Clauses. PhD, Indiana University.

Stowell, T.1989. "Subjects, Specifiers & X-bar Theory." In Alternative Conceptions of Phrase Structure. UCP, Chicago.

Wasow, T.1975. "Anaphoric Pronouns & Bound Variables." Language 51, 368-373.

Wikipedia

Wittgenstein, I.1958. Philosophical Investigations. Blackwell, Oxford.

Wright, W.1979. A Grammar of the Arabic Language. CUP, Cambridge.

"Hit me with your dagger and your sword but not with your word!"